ROBERT E. QUIRK is a graduate of Wayne State University and received his Ph.D. from Harvard. In 1961 he won the Bolton prize of the American Historical Association for *The Mexican Revolution, 1914-1915* and the American history prize of the Mississippi Valley Historical Association for *An Affair of Honor: Woodrow Wilson and the Occupation of Veracruz*. Both titles are available in Norton Library editions.

Mr. Quirk is a member of the history department at Indiana University.

ROBERT E. QUIRK

An Affair of
Honor

WOODROW WILSON AND
THE OCCUPATION OF VERACRUZ

The Norton Library
W · W · NORTON & COMPANY · INC ·
NEW YORK

Books That Live
The Norton imprint on a book means that in the publisher's
estimation it is a book not for a single season but for the years.
W. W. Norton & Company, Inc.

SBN 393 00390 6

Preface

As WOODROW WILSON took office in the spring of 1913, he announced that one of the chief objects of his administration was to "cultivate the friendship and deserve the confidence of our sister republics of Central and South America." This was part of the Wilsonian liberal program to "uphold the rights of man, [and] work for humanity and the happiness of men everywhere." It is ironic that this moral imperialism led the idealistic Wilson to use the club of armed intervention more frequently than any other American president. His biographers agree that his motives were exalted—and it is true that Veracruz, Santo Domingo, Haiti, and Nicaragua all benefited materially from American occupation. Roads were built. Sanitation was improved. Governments were freed from graft, and for the first time treasury accounts were balanced. Yet the gains were accompanied by the suspension of constitutions and the suppression of civil rights. Moreover, no sooner had the soldiers and marines departed than the subjected peoples forgot both honesty and efficiency in government and returned to their old ways.

This irony may explain the phenomenon so strange to many Americans: that Mexicans, in writing their histories, have been less bitter about the war with the United States in 1846 than the intervention in Veracruz in 1914. Even American historians agree that the War of 1846 was an aggressive act against Mexico—Americans desired Mexican territory and took it. Why, then, the more intense bitterness about the infinitely less damaging Veracruz occupation? To the Mexicans, Manifest Destiny was a harsh policy, but one which sprang from realistic and understandable motives. Wilson, however, clothed American aggression with the sanctimonious raiment of idealism. In insisting upon the morality of his acts, he aroused both the hatred and the scorn of the Mexicans—hatred over the invasion but a deep scorn for what they saw as his hypocrisy.

In this time of crisis it may be well for Americans to remember the nature of Woodrow Wilson's failures in his dealings with Latin Americans. As we view with dismay the consequences of the recent United States-sponsored invasion of Cuba—and as our government backs off to take a fresh start in our Latin American relations with the Alliance for Progress—we may profit from the realization that our failures today spring in part from the same attitudes displayed in 1914. There is still today the insistence upon the universal beneficence of the American brand of equality and individualism and on the superiority of American enterprise and technology. There also persists the urge to force these upon "backward peoples" whether they want them or not. And there is still present what Latin Americans have resented most about the United States—an insufferable air of superiority in our relations with others, even when we are trying to help them. There is no certainty that the Alliance for Progress will succeed. Indeed, there is the strong possibility that other Latin American countries will go the way of Castro's Cuba. We can be sure of one thing: If the problems of Latin Americans are to be solved, they must be solved in their own way and at their own pace. We may offer encouragement, friendship, understanding, and (when asked) counsel. But never tutelage, never superiority, never condescension. The proud peoples of Latin America will no more receive instruction from the men of Harvard than from the president of Princeton University.

Contents

	Preface	v
ONE:	*The Tampico Incident*	1
TWO:	*A Diplomatic Impasse*	34
THREE:	*Bloodshed at Veracruz*	78
FOUR:	*The Proconsuls*	121
FIVE:	*The Evacuation*	156
	Essay on Sources	173
	Index	179

ONE

The Tampico Incident

On April 21, 1914, United States military forces landed at Veracruz, Mexico, and occupied that port for more than six months. This act of hostility, President Woodrow Wilson said, was the direct result of the "studied contempt" of General Victoriano Huerta toward the American government and American nationals in Mexico. Specifically, it was in retaliation for three recent, but isolated incidents: the arrest of several American sailors and their commanding officer at Tampico on April 9; the detention of a mail courier at Veracruz on April 11; and the delay of an official dispatch of the Department of State, also on April 11, at Mexico City. We may think the causes picayune, and indeed they were, since all three were seen subsequently to be understandable mistakes. But war is a serious and dreadful business, and to commit a country to hostilities against a weaker neighbor requires sound reasons and self-justifications, if only to salve one's conscience. It is true that Wilson had not anticipated bloodshed at Veracruz; he had convinced himself that the Mexicans would not resist the landing. And he was appalled by the reports of loss of life at Veracruz—nineteen American sailors and several hundred Mexicans. But it was equally true that Wilson had been looking for just such an excuse to intervene in Mexico. His entire Mexican policy turned upon the elimination of Victoriano Huerta.

Woodrow Wilson and Victoriano Huerta came to the presidency of their respective countries almost simultaneously—Huerta preceded Wilson by somewhat less than two weeks. Yet if their terms of office began coincidently, the methods of their elevation were diametrically opposed. The American president was chosen by the free vote of the people, but the Mexican seized control of the government after a bloody revolution and the assassination of the legally elected president and vice president. Wilson never forgot the difference, nor would he permit Huerta to do so. From the moment of his inauguration he refused to recognize the regime of Huerta, who was, he said, a usurper and a murderer. To President Wilson, Huerta was the symbol for all that was wrong with Latin American governments. He offended Wilson's sense of decency and fair play, his desire to see popular and democratic rule installed everywhere. In entering the political arena Wilson had put aside his academic robes, but he could never shed the attitudes or the manner of an educator. In the fall of 1913 he told Sir William Tyrrell, the secretary of the British ambassador to Washington: "I am going to teach the South American republics to elect good men!"[1] The Latin Americans—and particularly the Mexicans—would be led by the nose into Zion, a Wilsonian political paradise bounded on one side by the ideals of the eighteenth century philosophers, on the other by stern Calvinistic piety. If Wilson's Mexican policy was a failure, which by all counts it was, it was precisely because he never lost his magisterial air

[1] Harley Notter, *The Origins of the Foreign Policy of Woodrow Wilson* (Baltimore, 1937), 274.

in dealing with those he considered his inferiors. The Mexicans would simply not be taught a lesson, and least of all by the president of the United States.

At a different time and under other circumstances, the incident at Tampico might have been passed off as the trivial event it obviously was. An apology by the local Mexican commander would have sufficed to erase this blot upon American honor. But the United States president's patience with Huerta—and Wilson never seemed patient— had worn thin. Eagerly he embraced the opportunity to hasten the overthrow of the Mexican president. This is not to suggest that Wilson was insincere. Yet he saw what he wanted to see in Mexico, believed what he wanted to believe, and in all of this was so certain of his own rectitude that no amount of argument would have swayed him. It is difficult, under the most favorable conditions, to deal satisfactorily with a zealot, and Huerta labored under a serious handicap in his relations with Wilson. The United States was powerful, Mexico weak and spent by revolutionary strife. American public opinion was squarely behind Wilson. Most Mexicans hated and despised Huerta. Above all, Huerta was not an effective administrator, not even a competent army commander. Once Wilson had decided upon his elimination, Huerta had no chance whatsoever.

Following Huerta's seizure of power and the death of President Francisco I. Madero in February, 1913, revolutionary groups took up arms throughout the Republic. In the south, Emiliano Zapata controlled the mountainous state of Morelos, defying Huerta as he had the national government of Madero. In the north, the opposition to Huerta coalesced around the figure of Venustiano Carranza, the governor of the state of Coahuila. As first chief of the Constitutionalist forces, Carranza won the allegiance of Francisco Villa and his Division of the North, of Alvaro Obregón's Army Corps of the Northwest, and of the Army

Corps of the Northeast under Pablo González. For nearly a year the Constitutionalists made little headway against Huerta, the months being spent in recruiting, outfitting, and training the revolutionary armies. Much of the equipment came from the United States. President William H. Taft had earlier declared an embargo against arms shipments to Mexico, and Wilson had permitted the ban to remain in effect through 1913. But the embargo had little effect so far as the Constitutionalists were concerned, for arms and ammunition were smuggled freely into Mexico at El Paso and other points along the frontier. Reputable American firms engaged in the profitable contraband trade across the border, while the customs agents winked at this supposedly illegal activity. After a year in office, Wilson lifted the ineffectual embargo and permitted the unhindered passage of arms to all factions, in a move calculated to hasten Huerta's downfall. If by early 1914 Villa's army was by far the most powerful in Mexico, it was in part because he had discovered a lucrative source of income on the ranches of Chihuahua. His men rounded up all the cattle they needed and sold them in the United States, using the dollars they received to purchase arms and supplies. Neither Obregón nor González could match Villa in this respect.

At no point in his campaign against the Constitutionalists did President Huerta take the initiative. Instead, he placed strong garrisons in the key railroad junctions of those lines which connected the north of Mexico with the capital: Torreón, Zacatecas, Saltillo, and Guadalajara. His armies were large; they were at least as well equipped as those of the various revolutionary chieftains. But the morale of his troops was low, and few cared to fight or die for Victoriano Huerta. Where most of the rebels had joined the revolution of their own volition, whether to fight idealistically for a cause or to gain plunder with a beloved leader, the government forces were by and large unwilling victims of the hated and dreaded *leva*. Federal ranks were filled by men coerced into service, many of them rounded up in cantinas, at bullfights, or at other public events and shipped like protesting cattle to the different commanders. It is not surprising that many broke and fled from battle with their first encounter with the enemy, nor that, given the opportunity, they would desert to the rebels.

By late March, 1914, three powerful Constitutionalist armies had begun to move south against the strategic positions held by Huerta's troops—Alvaro Obregón down the west coast, Francisco Villa in the center of the Republic, and Pablo González against Monterrey and Tampico. Huerta's days as president of Mexico were now numbered, and it was only a matter of time before Carranza occupied Mexico City—a matter of time, that is, and of great destruction of property and loss of life. It was to avoid these last that Wilson took the steps which led to American intervention in Mexico. He was at all times scrupulous, however, to place the responsibility for the intervention squarely upon the shoulders of Victoriano Huerta.

For the Constitutionalists it was the most critical moment of their revolution against Huerta. In the last week of March, Villa's Division of the North battered the approaches to Torreón, which dominated the cotton-producing area of the Comarca Lagunera. By April 2 he had taken the city and cut up a large federal army. There was now no Huertista force, short of Mexico City, capable of halting Villa's army. Yet in the hour of imminent victory an ominous crack appeared in the facade of the Constitutionalist revolution. Villa began to demonstrate an independence of spirit which was completely unacceptable to Venustiano Carranza, the civilian head of the revolutionary government. Since Villa now controlled the cotton country, as well as the mining and ranching areas of Chihuahua, it behooved Carranza to take Tampico and the surrounding oilfields. At the same time, he sought to hinder Villa's march south by diverting his army against Saltillo, which was still held by the federals. In this way, Carranza hoped, Obregón or González might reach Mexico City before Villa. Both Obregón and González were completely loyal to their first chief.[2]

Before 1900, though it was Mexico's second ranking port, Tampico was scarcely more than a large village. The roads to the interior were narrow and unpaved, and undulated through sandhills or around marshes, through dank tropical forests to the lofty central plateau, or up the twisting valleys of the Pánuco River and its tributaries to tiny and unimportant Indian settlements. The paucity of trade into the interior did not warrant the expenditure of funds by the national or local governments to maintain these roads in good condition. Tampico was built on the northern bank of the Pánuco River, about ten miles inland, just where the crook of its elbow makes a sharp turn up to the sea. Because it was inland, there was some protection from the tropical storms and hurricanes which lashed the coast of the Mexican gulf each summer.

In the first years of the twentieth century, the discovery of oil turned Tampico into a boomtown. Almost overnight the population doubled, tripled, quintupled, until it approached 30,000. The foreign colony, mostly Americans, was exceeded in size only by that of Mexico City, the national capital. Mexico became one of the world's leading producers of crude and refined petroleum, and foreign wealth poured into the country, as American and British companies vied for concessions from the governments of Porfirio Díaz and his revolutionary successor, Francisco I. Madero. Railroads were laid to Victoria and

---

[2] Robert E. Quirk, *The Mexican Revolution, 1914-1915* (Bloomington, Indiana, 1960), 18-34.

Monterrey in the north and to Valles and San Luis Potosí
—and hence to Mexico City—in the west and south. Along
both sides of the river at Tampico, storage tanks grew like
mushrooms; pipelines from Tampico reached into the oilfields to siphon out the raw petroleum. At Arbol Grande,
Waters-Pierce, a Standard Oil subsidiary, constructed a
refinery to produce gasoline. By 1914 the area around
Tampico was the richest in the Republic and a valuable
prize for any faction, whether that of Victoriano Huerta
or the Constitutionalist revolutionaries of Carranza.

In Tampico, General Ignacio Morelos Zaragoza, military
governor of the state of Tamaulipas and commander of the
federal garrison, could count on about 2,000 troops to
defend the port against the Constitutionalists. In addition,
he controlled the federalized state guard of Tamaulipas.
But these were of even poorer quality than the national
army; they had almost no military training and no sense
of discipline. Though Morelos Zaragoza publicly expressed
his confidence in the outcome of the impending battle, his
optimism was unfounded. Tampico was a most difficult
site to defend. To the north and east there were rolling
hills which came up to the outskirts of the city. Moreover, these hills were covered with a shrubby vegetation
which provided an excellent concealment for the attacking forces. In order to hold off the Constitutionalists, the
federal troops needed to take up positions farther out on
the rail line to Victoria, beyond Arbol Grande and Doña
Cecilia, to dig trenches and to construct strong emplace-
ments for their fieldpieces. But Morelos Zaragoza made no
attempt to do this, limiting his efforts to the defense of the
city proper. In the river the federal gunboat *Veracruz*
could offer some assistance by firing upon the rebel positions. Since it was inconceivable that a pitched battle at
Tampico would not endanger American lives and properties, the naval commander and the diplomatic represen-

tative of the United States at the port took immediate steps to limit the area of the impending conflict.[3]

Vessels of the United States navy had been stationed at both Tampico and Veracruz for several months. It was not unusual in that era to find warships in foreign ports to protect American nationals, but the large number kept in Mexican coastal waters in 1914 was intended by Wilson also to be a constant reminder to the government of Mexico of his displeasure with Huerta. Rear Admiral Frank F. Fletcher commanded the Fourth Division of the Atlantic Fleet based at Veracruz, while Henry T. Mayo, also a rear admiral, was in command of the Fifth Division at Tampico. There was no fixed number of ships at either port. Instead, they were shuttled back and forth by Mayo and Fletcher as the occasion demanded.

In the event of an emergency at Tampico, Mayo was required by difficulties of communication to act upon his own initiative (or perhaps to consult Fletcher), for he had no means of reaching the Navy Department in the United States either by radio or telegraph. Though Admiral Fletcher was not Mayo's immediate superior (for they held equal command), all of the dispatches from Tampico to the department were sent through Fletcher at Veracruz to the land stations at Key West. Naval radio transmission and reception in 1914 were quite haphazard. This was before the advent of the radio tube and the Armstrong circuit, and the successful transmission of spark signals depended upon the height and complexity of the sending and receiving antennas and the time of day the messages were sent out. The radio signals of the older battleships, with their short masts, carried only two or three hundred

[3] Henry T. Mayo to Frank F. Fletcher, March 28, 1914, Navy Files, National Archives, Record Group 45/659 (hereafter cited as RG 45); Clarence Miller to Mayo, March 29, 1914, State Department Files, National Archives, Post Records (Tampico) 800/658 (hereafter cited as PRT 800); Mayo to Fletcher, April 7, 1914, RG 45/659.

miles under the most favorable conditions. And even on the latest American dreadnoughts the height of the antennas was limited by the necessity of passing under the Brooklyn Bridge into the naval yard at New York. Fletcher on *Florida,* a newer vessel, could reach Key West only at night, and then it was impossible to get through a long coded message because of the static.[4] As it was, most naval commanders were accustomed to act without consulting Washington (as had George Dewey at Manila), and Mayo was no exception. When Mayo was sent to Tampico, Admiral B. A. Fiske, chief of naval operations, asked Fletcher for his estimation of his new associate. Fletcher's reply was both prescient and revealing: "What may happen may never have happened before. The man on the spot has only his judgment for a guide. I am pleased that Mayo is here now."[5]

Mayo was 57 years of age in 1914, and he had been in the navy for more than forty of these. He was only 15 when he came to the Naval Academy at Annapolis, and 19 when he received his commission and was assigned to his first sea duty aboard the monitor *Tennessee.* His rise through the ranks was slow in a service which equated rank and ability with age. By 1903, Mayo was a captain in command of the Mare Island Navy Yard in California. He had gained a reputation as a "coaster"—that is, he preferred duty on the more pleasant California coast. When Wilson's new secretary of the navy, Josephus Daniels, made a tour of inspection of the country's naval establishments, he was so impressed by Mayo's capabilities that he brought him to Washington to be his aide for personnel and secured his promotion, over older and more experienced officers, to rear admiral. Mayo soon wearied of his desk duty, however,

[4] General Board to Navy Department, June 7, 1913, Navy Files, Alexandria, Va., General Board Records 419 (hereafter cited as GBR).
[5] Fletcher to B. A. Fiske, February 3, 1914, Josephus Daniels Papers, Library of Congress, Box 39.

and requested reassignment with a squadron. Daniels agreed, but first sent him to the Naval War College at Newport, Rhode Island, for further study. On December 26, 1913, Mayo assumed command of the Fourth Division and was ordered to Mexican waters.[6]

Mayo's features reflected his personality. His face seemed chiseled from granite. He had sandy hair, deep-set steel blue eyes, a prominent nose, and a firm jaw, thrust forward like the prow of a man-of-war. His scraggly mustache made him appear older than he actually was. He was an obdurate naval officer, accustomed to giving orders and to seeing them carried out with dispatch. A friend described Mayo: "He impresses you the moment he speaks as a man of business and action. He does what he thinks is right, and as a rule he does not lose a lot of time doing it. And he never quibbles or hesitates once he makes up his mind what the right course is to pursue."[7] This was the man who saw the dangerous situation developing at Tampico. He would do all in his power to protect American lives and interests. If necessary, Mayo was prepared to land armed forces to prevent trouble.

There were two battleships under Mayo's command at Tampico, *Connecticut* and *Minnesota,* the former flying the admiral's flag. Neither was a new ship, and both were classified by the navy in 1914 as secondline vessels. Although the two battleships carried marine detachments, and the sailors of the ship's companies could be used in an emergency for a landing, Mayo was at a great disadvantage at Tampico, for neither ship could enter the river. The Pánuco itself was deep enough to float the larger ships, but a sandbar across the mouth of the river prevented the passage, even at high tide, of ships with a draft of more than 21 feet. Mayo also had two cruisers, *Chester* and

    [6] "Mayo at Tampico," *Literary Digest,* XLVIII (May 2, 1914), 1056-1057, 1060; *New York Times,* April 19, 1914, VI, 5:1-8; April 21, 1914, 3:6.
    [7] *Literary Digest,* XLVIII, 1060.

Des Moines, which could negotiate the entrance to the river with ease and could be anchored at Tampico. *San Francisco,* a mine depot ship, might be used in a critical situation, for it had a mean draft of less than 19 feet. But it would have been a tricky and highly dangerous maneuver. The bottom of the river, on the north side of the bar, was littered with concrete blocks dislodged from an old unrepaired jetty which protected the entrance.[8]

Anticipating trouble with the approach of the Constitutionalists, Mayo requested Fletcher on March 28 to send him the gunboat *Dolphin* for use as his headquarters inside the river. *Dolphin* had had a venerable career; it was one of the first vessels built for the "New Navy" after 1883, and during the two terms of Grover Cleveland it had been used as a presidential yacht. When the vessel arrived at Tampico, Mayo transferred his flag from *Connecticut* and anchored the gunboat inside the river in order to keep close surveillance over the events ashore. Day by day small boats carrying his messages made frequent shuttle trips between *Dolphin* and *Connecticut,* as Mayo reported to Fletcher by radio the gradually accelerating advance of the rebel forces. In addition to the American naval vessels at Tampico, there were also two other foreign cruisers in the river, the German *Dresden* and the British *Hermione.* These would, it was hoped, protect the interests of their own nationals in the area.[9]

Until March 25 the Constitutionalists contented themselves with small attacks against the rail line linking Tampico with Valles and San Luis Potosí. Still the trains, guarded by federal troops, continued to get through and brought in more reinforcements for the garrison of Morelos Zaragoza. The main body of the rebels, under General Luis

[8] War Portfolio No. 1, Information Section (Mexico), GBR.
[9] Mayo to Fletcher, March 28, 1914, RG 45/659; *New York Times,* April 19, 1914, VI, 5:1-8; Miller, "Political Conditions at Tampico," May 21, 1914, PRT 800/1089.

Caballeros, had taken control of the tracks from Victoria
to choke off all communications north of Tampico. On
March 26, Caballeros' advance guard reached Laguna
Puerta, a small station about ten miles from Tampico, and
set up a headquarters there. From Laguna Puerta, groups
of skirmishers probed the defense points along the railroad
and automobile road into Tampico, though there was no
sustained attack. The rebels lacked fieldpieces, and they
did not wish to hazard an all-out battle for the city until
their three-inch guns had arrived. The presence of the large
Constitutionalist force so near to Tampico caused grave
alarm within the city. The American naval and diplomatic
officials hurried plans for the possible evacuation of the
foreign population.[10]

The danger of numerous casualties was evident if gunfire
should ignite any of the oil or gasoline tanks in Arbol Grande
or Doña Cecilia. There was a brief engagement near Doña
Cecilia on March 27, and the federal gunboat *Veracruz* fired
a number of shells in the general direction of the Constitutionalists. At the request of Clarence Miller, the American consul at Tampico, Mayo sent a steamer down the river
to Doña Cecilia to bring the American women and children
into Tampico. All preferred to stay with their families until
the danger was more apparent. For the Americans in the
area the petroleum properties represented not only a capital
investment of millions of dollars, but livelihoods, homes,
and friendships as well. Many Americans in Mexico were
already critical of Wilson's seeming endorsement of the
rebel factions. The best hope for law and order in Mexico
—and the protection of foreign interests—lay, they felt, with
Huerta, not the Constitutionalists. For them the revolutionary cause was equated with the savagery of Francisco
Villa and Emiliano Zapata. The Americans at Tampico,

---

[10] Mayo to Fletcher, March 28, 1914, RG 45/659; Miller to Mayo, March
29, 1914, PRT 800/658.

as in the rest of Mexico, expected that the naval forces would be used to protect their properties against rebel attacks, not to evacuate women and children. So they delayed leaving until the last possible moment, hoping almost against hope for military intervention.[11]

Inside Tampico, many business establishments prepared for the inevitable street fighting that would accompany any attack on the city. Two banks brought their specie deposits aboard the German cruiser *Dresden* for safekeeping. Merchants and jewelers packed up their small valuables, in anticipation of a hasty exodus. They did not trust the Constitutionalist soldiers—probably with reason, for any city captured by the rebels could expect a sacking as a matter of course. The federal troops spent the next several days strengthening their lines northeast of the city and digging trenches in preparation for the rebel attacks. It was clear that the battle for Tampico would take place in the area facing Arbol Grande and Doña Cecilia. Admiral Mayo reported to Fletcher on March 28 that the federals were refusing "passage through their lines to everyone."[12]

The next week at Tampico passed in calm expectancy. From time to time the nights—and less frequently the daylight hours—were punctuated by rifle shots or a staccato of machinegun fire. In reply, *Veracruz* and *Zaragoza* (another federal gunboat, which had brought reinforcements into Tampico on March 31) lofted shrapnel shells toward the rebel encampment. The failure of the Constitutionalists to answer the gunboats in kind indicated that they had not as yet received their cannons from Pablo González. There was no panic in Tampico. Except for the closed shops, the town maintained its usual appearance, much as though no battle were pending. The three American ships in the river sent parties of sailors ashore each day to play base-

11 Mayo to Fletcher, March 28, 1914, RG 45/659.
12 Mayo to Fletcher, March 28, 1914, RG 45/659.

ball. Relations between the Americans and the federal forces were good. Each time a vessel stood in or out of the port, the ships exchanged salutes. (Technically this was contrary to American navy regulations, which forbade salutes for a country whose government was not recognized by the United States.) On April 2, at the request of the Mexicans, *Dolphin* hoisted the Mexican colors at the main and fired twenty-one gun salvos at sunrise, noon, and sunset to commemorate the capture of Puebla by General Porfirio Díaz from the French in 1867. The American families at the refineries remained in their homes, still making no attempt to take refuge in Tampico or aboard the vessels in the river.[13]

On the morning of April 5 the expected storm broke. In the hours before dawn there was heavy firing from the rebels along the road between Altamira and Doña Cecilia, and during the day, dead and wounded federal soldiers were carried into Tampico in increasing numbers. The watch officers aboard the naval vessels could see the stretchers and wagons brought along the railroad tracks northeast of the city. Fearing that there would soon be fighting in the area of the petroleum properties, Admiral Mayo—in collaboration with the German and British naval commanders—drew up a letter to be presented to the federal and rebel leaders. He assured both Caballeros and Morelos Zaragoza that the United States forces would remain neutral. But he reserved the right, he said, "to take all necessary steps" to protect American lives and properties. At no time did Mayo consult Fletcher about his plans, nor did he ask for instructions from Washington.[14]

On the following morning the Constitutionalists made a heavy attack along the entire river front north of Tampico.

[13] Logs of *Dolphin, Chester, Des Moines,* March 27 to April 4, 1914, Navy Files, National Archives.
[14] Mayo to Fletcher, April 7, 1914, RG 45/659; Mayo to Federal and Constitutionalist Commanders, April 5, 1914, PRT 800/661.

The few federal troops there put up no resistance and hastily withdrew, permitting the rebels to occupy La Barra, Doña Cecilia, and Arbol Grande. *Veracruz* now moved down the river to shell the enemy forces who had taken up positions behind the oil tanks. It was time for Mayo to act. Hoping to avoid destruction of the refinery, he sent Lieutenant Commander Ralph K. Earle, *Dolphin's* captain, to present his letter to Morelos Zaragoza. The federal commander depreciated the Constitutionalist attack, assuring Earle that the rebels were still without artillery. It was his opinion that they had entered Doña Cecilia only to get food and that they would soon leave. He did promise the Americans, however, that *Veracruz* and *Zaragoza* would not fire into the refinery. Earle asked permission to send an officer through the federal lines to carry a similar message to Caballeros, but Morelos Zaragoza replied that he could not accede to such a request on his own initiative, that he must consult his superiors in Mexico City. When Earle reported to the admiral, Mayo decided not to wait (the request was subsequently denied by the Mexican Ministry of War), for it was a simple matter for the Americans to land a boat at Doña Cecilia and bring the letter directly to the Constitutionalists. Colonel Emiliano J. Nafarrete, in charge of the rebels' advance troops, confirmed the reports that he had no artillery, but he assured Mayo that when his guns did arrive, he would seek to avoid a bombardment of Tampico.[15]

Once more Mayo sent boats to Doña Cecilia and Arbol Grande, asking the Americans there to come into Tampico. If necessary, he said, they could come aboard the naval vessels in the river, whenever the fighting became too intense in the city. Again no one would come. Instead, the Americans at the refinery requested him to land forces

---

[15] Mayo to Fletcher, April 7, 1914, RG 45/659; Miller to Mayo, April 6, 1914, PRT 800/663; Miller, "Political Conditions."

to protect the oil properties. Mayo replied that to do so would constitute interference in the hostilities between the two forces, because the rebels occupied positions behind the tanks. Upon his further insistence, several boatloads of Americans were brought into Tampico. Inside the city, Miller and other consular officials posted public announcements, warning all foreigners to be prepared to come aboard the ships at a moment's notice. During the night a number of warehouses belonging to a German company were set afire in Doña Cecilia, but fortunately none of the oil tanks was ignited.[16]

Early on April 7 the rebels made a surprise attack on the outskirts of Tampico near the Iturbide Bridge. This bridge spanned a canal connecting the marshy Laguna del Carpentero with the Pánuco River and marked the northeastern boundary of the city. Actually it was nothing more than a trestle of the rail line from Victoria, but the bridge was of undoubted importance to the federal troops, since the expected main assault of the Constitutionalists would come at that point. The rebels, having crept up to the bridge through the dense bushes which lined the canal, suddenly fired into the city. When the federal troops guarding the position returned their fire, the Constitutionalists withdrew to their previously held positions among the bluffs overlooking Arbol Grande.[17]

During the skirmish, many foreigners fled to the consulates for protection. When it became evident that the rebels had not begun an all-out attack on the city, they returned to their homes. Throughout the day, *Veracruz* shelled the rebel positions, and one of the shells hit an oil tank at Arbol Grande, setting it afire. Though the flames did not leap to the other tanks, the dense black smoke

[16] Mayo to Fletcher, April 7, 1914, RG 45/659; Miller, "Political Conditions."

[17] *Dolphin* Log, April 7, 1914; Mayo to Fletcher, April 7, 1914, RG 45/659.

was visible for miles up and down the river. There was now a marked influx of refugees from the rebel-held areas, and for the first time large numbers of foreigners began to go aboard the naval vessels. In the evening, *Zaragoza* returned from Veracruz with reinforcements for the federal garrison in Tampico, and the next day a commercial liner, *Libertad,* docked with three hundred more men. Though he was seriously weakening the forces at Veracruz, Huerta was determined to hold Tampico at all cost.[18]

There were numerous skirmishes on April 8, with the rebels again attacking along the canal near the Iturbide Bridge. In the course of the day American naval launches were busy, bringing in refugees from points above and below the city. As the cruisers became crowded with civilians, Mayo ordered *Des Moines* to carry them to the two battleships anchored outside the river. But strong north winds had sprung up during the afternoon, and the cruisers were unable to cross the bar. Until the storm had spent itself, all of the ships would remain in the river. Because so few refugees could be accommodated aboard the cruisers, and it was evident now that the rebels had not yet begun their main attack, Mayo sent all of the Americans ashore to find refuge in Tampico.[19]

As hundreds of refugees crowded into hotels or private homes, both Mayo and Clarence Miller took an increasingly serious view of the situation. Miller radioed an urgent request to the United States State Department to send an army transport to Tampico, or, if that was not feasible, to charter a commercial vessel, perhaps one of the Ward Line steamers at Veracruz, to evacuate the Americans. William Jennings Bryan, the secretary of state, after consultation with President Wilson, refused. He told Miller that the

[18] Miller, "Political Conditions"; Mayo to Fletcher, April 7, 1914, RG 45/659.

[19] Miller, "Political Conditions"; Mayo to Fletcher, April 7, 1914 (date letter was started, not sent), RG 45/659; *Dolphin* Log, April 8, 1914.

navy ships then at Tampico must suffice. Both Bryan and Wilson showed a curious lack of concern for the safety of American nationals throughout Mexico, whether at Tampico, or with the mining companies of Chihuahua, or in commerce in the capital. Wilson told his personal physician, Dr. Cary Grayson: "I sometimes have to pause and remind myself that I am president of the whole United States and not merely of a few property holders in the Republic of Mexico." He would not consider using armed forces to protect either lives or property anywhere. Instead, he advised those Americans in the critical areas to leave Mexico until the danger was over.[20]

On the evening of the eighth an incident took place at Tampico which might have had serious consequences. A marine courier from the American consulate was detained near the Iturbide Bridge by federal troops and sent to Morelos Zaragoza under arrest. He was clearly an American, but his detention was indicative of the uneasy state of mind of the defenders of the bridge. The man was returned to his ship, and Mayo accepted the explanation of the federal commander. He told Morelos Zaragoza that the marine had "very stupidly" become lost while carrying a message from the consulate to the ships moored at the fiscal wharf. Mayo did not count the incident important enough to pursue further.[21] It was a bizarre affair, however, for the bridge was nowhere near the fiscal wharf; it was, in fact, in the opposite direction. Miller may have been attempting to get a message through the federal lines to the Con-

[20] Miller to William W. Canada, April 8, 1914, Navy Files, National Archives, *Dolphin* Record Signal Book; William J. Bryan to Canada, April 11, 1914, State Department Files, National Archives, 812.00/11454 (unless otherwise indicated, all correspondence of the Department of State will be from the 812.00 files and will be identified only by the slash number); Cary T. Grayson, *Woodrow Wilson: An Intimate Memoir* (New York, 1960), 30.

[21] Ignacio Morelos Zaragoza to Mayo, April 8, 1914, RG 45/659; Mayo to Morelos Zaragoza, April 8, 1914, RG 45/659.

stitutionalist troops; this would explain the failure of Mayo to take a sterner attitude concerning the arrest. It is worth noting that this was the precise point at which the much graver incident of the following day occurred.

The morning of April 9 at Tampico was gray and cool, unseasonably cool for so late in the year. Brisk northerly winds, the aftermath of the previous day's storm, kept the gunboats and cruisers bottled up in the river. *Dolphin* was still anchored at the fiscal wharf. Ashore, there were several short bursts of rifle fire, while intermittently the two federal gunboats tossed shells into the rebel positions at Doña Cecilia and Arbol Grande. But the populace of Tampico was granted a brief respite, for there was no attack there, as there had been on the previous two days. The ordinary citizens went about their appointed tasks in the market, the plaza, or the shops. Most businesses remained closed, however, with their facades protected by iron gates or bars. The federal troops were alert. They did not venture beyond the confines of the city. Still they knew that an attack was inevitable—if not today, perhaps tomorrow; if not tomorrow, then next week. Whenever the rebels got their cannons, there would be a major assault upon Tampico, and it would doubtless come precisely at the point where the northern railroad entered the city, that is, at the Iturbide Bridge.[22]

The many trips required of the small naval boats in the river in relaying messages between *Dolphin* and the ships at anchor outside, and in bringing in refugees from various points along the river, had virtually exhausted the supply of gasoline carried in the American vessels. No fuel could be purchased from any of the accustomed sources, the American companies in Arbol Grande and Doña Cecilia, for these had been closed during the recent rebel attacks.

[22] *Dolphin* Log, April 9, 1914; Mayo to Fletcher, April 7, 1914, RG 45/659; Miller, "Political Conditions."

Needing gasoline soon, Captain Earle went ashore to the American consulate to ask if Miller knew of any supplies in Tampico. Quite by chance there was a German civilian, Max Tyron, in the consul's office, and he offered to sell several cans which were stored, he said, in his warehouse on the canal northeast of the city. He gave his address and the location of the warehouse to Captain Earle.[23]

Upon his return to the ship, Earle ordered his young assistant paymaster to take a whaleboat and crew to Tyron's dock to pick up the gasoline. He pointed out the exact location of the warehouse on a large map of the city, indicating the route down the river and up the narrow canal. Earle was evidently unaware, or perhaps it did not seem important to him, that the warehouse was less than a hundred yards from the railroad and the Iturbide Bridge, and very close to the federals' first line of defense. American boats had been plying back and forth between all points on the river, and there had been no difficulty before. But this was the first time since hostilities had begun in the area that an American naval vessel had been sent into the canal. As a precaution, the whaleboat flew the colors fore and aft.[24]

It was purely a routine mission; no one thought it important enough to mark the boat's departure in the ship's log. Instead, in the precise hand of the senior watch officer, Ensign Harold Terry Bartlett, there was recorded the provisioning of the mess: ice, ham, onions, and sweet potatoes. At the end of his watch, almost as an afterthought, Ensign Bartlett wrote: "Max Tyron reports the arrest of the whaleboat's crew."[25]

That was all; to the crew, to the officers of the gunboat,

23 Ralph T. Earle to Mayo, April 9, 1914, RG 45/659; Miller, "Political Conditions."
24 Earle to Mayo, April 9, 1914, RG 45/659; Mayo to Fletcher, April 7, 1914, RG 45/659; Fletcher to Josephus Daniels, April 11, 1914 /11988.
25 *Dolphin* Log, April 9, 1914.

the incident did not seem the stuff of which great issues are made, and certainly not a *casus belli*.

The assistant paymaster was Ensign Charles C. Copp. He was 23 years of age, and had been a commissioned officer for only two years. Most of that time, moreover, had been spent in the United States at a desk job, and this was his first tour of duty at sea. His work was still primarily clerical. Yet it did not appear to be an onerous mission for any officer, even one as inexperienced as Ensign Copp. He dropped the boat into the river and secured a hitch to a steam launch. Then he and his men were towed to the mouth of the canal, where their whaleboat was cast loose. On the left bank of the canal they could see several warehouses with wooden docks jutting into the dark, torpid water. The right bank was choked with vegetation, for the city did not extend beyond the canal. There was no activity on either side of the canal, and the only sounds came from the oars as they cut through the water. Without difficulty the men reached Tyron's dock and tied the boat alongside his old lighter. Under the direction of Copp and Max Tyron, they carried the cans of gasoline from the warehouse, stowing them in the whaleboat. Two men, Coxswain G. H. Siefert and Seaman J. P. Harrington, remained in the boat.[26]

Tyron lived in the first house on Calle Altamira. He was one block from the railroad track, and his warehouse was the eastern point of a triangle formed by Altamira, the railroad right-of-way, and the canal, which ran diagonally to the northwest. At the bridge the troops of Morelos Zaragoza were alert, anxiously scanning the bushes on the other side of the canal. A small motorboat patrolled the canal, on the lookout for any sign of the enemy. The presence of uniformed men with a boat so close to the

[26] Statement of Charles C. Copp to Earle, April 9, 1914, RG 45/659; Statement of Max Tyron to Earle, April 9, 1914, RG 45/659.

bridge could not have passed unnoticed, and as the American sailors loaded the gasoline, Max Tyron noted that a federal officer aboard the motorboat had observed their activity. He did not think it sufficiently important, however, to mention the matter to Ensign Copp. Within a few minutes a squad of soldiers, armed with rifles, appeared at the warehouse to investigate. The Mexican officer ordered the sailors to cease loading the boat. Neither Copp nor his men could speak Spanish, but there was no mistaking the import of his gestures. Siefert and Harrington were still in the boat, stowing the cans of gasoline in the hold. The federal officer gestured for them to come ashore. When they hesitated and looked to Copp for direction, the Mexican barked an order. The soldiers leveled their rifles at the men's breasts. Ensign Copp then told the two men to obey the orders, and Siefert and Harrington joined the others at the warehouse. Surrounded by the riflemen, they were all led down the street. None of the Americans was armed. They put up no resistance. Nor did they seek to remonstrate. But the two on the whaleboat, Siefert and Harrington, had been taken at gunpoint from a naval vessel flying the American colors.[27]

As they were leaving, Max Tyron, who was fluent in Spanish, protested the arrest of the Americans to the federal officer. The Mexican replied that he had no choice, that his orders were to permit no one in that area without a pass. He could not release the prisoners, he said, without consulting his superiors. Tyron was acquainted with the Mexican officers at the bridge (they were all citizens of Tampico and members of the state guard of Tamaulipas), and he was given permission to report the matter to the military governor, Morelos Zaragoza. Meanwhile, the Americans were marched under guard a short distance up Calle Altamira, across the railroad track, to the headquarters of

[27] Statements of Copp and Tyron.

Colonel Ramón H. Hinojosa, commander of the federal troops in that sector of Tampico. Through an interpreter, Hinojosa told Ensign Copp that he and his men had no business in that area, which was under military control. Within a few minutes the Americans were returned to the dock to resume their loading. They were not molested in any way, or insulted by their guard or Colonel Hinojosa. Nor was public notice taken of their arrest and detention. The incident had occurred in a residential area, far from the busy plazas of Tampico. Few, if any, of the civilians in the city were aware of the event at all. Though the men were given permission to load the gasoline, they were detained at the warehouse until orders for their release could come from Morelos Zaragoza.[28]

Max Tyron did not go to the headquarters of the federal commander. Instead he proceeded immediately to the fiscal wharf where *Dolphin* was tied up to report the incident to Captain Earle. When Admiral Mayo, also aboard *Dolphin,* learned of the arrest, he directed Earle to lodge a strong protest with Morelos Zaragoza and to secure the release of the men. Captain Earle stopped at the American consulate to pick up Miller so that he would have an interpreter. According to Miller, the military governor was "dumbfounded" when he was informed of the incident. He apologized profusely to the Americans and made no effort to justify the actions of his men. They were not regular soldiers, he explained, but members of the state guard, who were "evidently ignorant of the first laws of war." Morelos Zaragoza was completely sincere, and at no time did Earle seem inclined to magnify the arrest into an international incident. Clarence Miller was convinced that the apology had been accepted and that the matter had been closed. He wrote later to the American secretary of state: "If I had known otherwise, and if someone had suggested

[28] Statements of Copp and Tyron.

to me that [Morelos Zaragoza] should send some officers of high rank off to make an apology and explanation to the admiral, I would have suggested to him that course of action, and I have no doubt but that he would gladly have done so."[29]

It is probable that Morelos Zaragoza saw no difference between this incident and the arrest of the marine courier on the previous day. And in that case the explanation of the federal commander had been accepted by Admiral Mayo without question. There was no inkling of impending trouble in the demeanor of either Miller or Captain Earle when they confronted the Mexican commander. By the time Earle had returned to the waterfront, he could see the heavily laden whaleboat already proceeding up the river to the fiscal wharf, painfully making its way against the current. About an hour had passed since the arrest of the sailors.

Upon their return, the men were interviewed by Captain Earle, who also took a statement from Max Tyron. Although the stories differed slightly in some details, in essence all of those involved corroborated each other: The two men had been ordered from the whaleboat at gunpoint while the boat flew the American flag; and they had been marched a short distance (the estimates varied) into Tampico. Ensign Copp reported to Mayo personally. The young ensign was upbraided by the admiral for permitting his men to be removed from the boat. But Copp protested that at the time he felt he had no choice, that twelve rifles pointed at the men warranted his action.[30]

Whatever Miller and Earle had thought at the time, the incident was not closed by the apology of Morelos Zaragoza. Although the federal commander saw it in the same

---

[29] *Dolphin* Log, April 9, 1914; Earle to Mayo, April 9, 1914, RG 45/659; Mayo to Fletcher, April 7 [*sic*], 1914, RG 45/659; Fletcher to Daniels, April 11, 1914 /11988; Miller, "Political Conditions."
[30] Copp to author, March 6, 1958.

light as the arrest of the marine courier, Mayo did not. To him a vessel—even a whaleboat—flying the American colors was sovercign territory of the United States. Moreover, the arrest had become public and arrant, he felt, when the sailors were marched through the streets of the city (it is important to note, however, that none of the men had ever said that their arrest had been observed by civilians), and because of this the apology, no matter how sincere, did not suffice. Mayo was determined that the reparation be made as open as he believed the insult to have been. In the instant of that decision, Mayo gave the affair international significance. It was no longer a simple matter between two military commanders to be settled amicably by an exchange of courteous letters. Morelos Zaragoza must apologize, not to Admiral Mayo, but to the United States, for what Mayo deemed was an infringement upon the sovereignty of his country.

The decision was Mayo's, made without reference to higher authority. He did not even report his action to Fletcher until 5 p.m. that afternoon, although many other less important messages were sent to Veracruz by Mayo's radio operator. In any event, President Wilson sustained Mayo's demands and never raised the point of irresponsibility on Mayo's part. It is clear that the admiral, in his demands, did not ask a factfinding, but rather a punishment, and his inflexibility placed the Mexicans in a difficult position. They were being judged without a hearing, condemned without a trial. Nor did Mayo foresee the results of his action—military threats and finally the seizure of Veracruz. It is obvious that he believed that he could handle the matter locally, that he need not trouble Washington with such trivialities.

Mayo sent a strong note to Morelos Zaragoza in which he rejected the oral apologies as insufficient. He recited the events as they had been reported to him by Ensign Copp.

"I do not need to tell you," he wrote, "that taking men from a boat flying the American flag is a hostile act, not to be excused." Mayo rejected the plea that Hinojosa had acted in ignorance: "Responsibility for hostile acts cannot be avoided by a plea of ignorance." "In view of the publicity of this occurrence," he said, "I must require that you send me, by suitable members of your staff, a formal disavowal of and an apology for the act, together with your assurance that the officer responsible for it will receive severe punishment. Also that you hoist the American flag in a prominent position on shore and salute it with 21 guns, which salute will be duly returned by this ship." Mayo demanded that Morelos Zaragoza's answer be in his hands and the salute fired within twenty-four hours.[31]

Admiral Mayo was resolved to make the presentation of his demands an impressive occasion, so that the Mexican commander would not take them lightly. He ordered the note delivered by Commander William A. Moffett, senior officer of the vessels in the river and captain of the cruiser *Chester*. Moffett was in full uniform and wearing sidearms, accompanied by aides, as he confronted Morelos Zaragoza. The federal commander was surprised that his oral apologies had not been accepted and was deeply disturbed by the severity of the reparation now required. In his reply to Mayo he stressed that he could not comply without first consulting his superiors in Mexico City. Mayo quickly agreed to a 24-hour delay in the execution of his demands, though he did not retire any of them or lessen their severity. So far as he was concerned, the Mexicans at Tampico would salute the American colors and would punish Colonel Hinojosa, or he would take punitive action against them. What that action would be he did not say, and probably was not prepared as yet for that eventuality. When he finally informed Fletcher in Veracruz of his ultimatum,

[31] Mayo to Morelos Zaragoza, April 9, 1914, RG 45/659.

his colleague agreed completely. Fletcher felt that if the salute were not fired, Mayo would be justified in seizing one of the federal gunboats in the river.[32]

In Tampico, Consul Miller was appalled by the turn of events. Miller had the practical point of view of the experienced foreign service officer faced with frequent trouble between Mexicans and Americans. Just the week before, several American civilians in Tampico had been taken into custody by the federals, charged with furnishing aid to the Constitutionalists. Miller had settled the matter on the spot by conferring with Morelos Zaragoza and had thus easily secured the release of all those arrested. Miller believed in this new instance that Mayo's demands were excessive, that the first apology of Morelos Zaragoza should have sufficed. He saw no difference between the arrest of sailors and the arrest of civilians. Yet though he disagreed with Mayo, he had no way of voicing his disapproval. An admiral had more authority and prestige than a consul, however experienced. Miller could not even communicate his opinions to the American State Department. All diplomatic dispatches to Washington were sent through Mayo's radio to Veracruz, to be relayed through the Department of the Navy to the secretary of state. Once the salute was demanded, Miller sent out almost nothing, and he was virtually isolated from State Department directions, for the navy had now, in effect, superseded the diplomatic service in handling relations with the Mexicans at Tampico. It was not until late in May, when the Constitutionalists had finally captured Tampico, that Miller telegraphed a long report to Bryan in which he expressed his dissident views very strongly. This was, of course, long after the event.[33]

Mayo's dispatch to Admiral Fletcher at 5 p.m., April 9, carried the barest details concerning the incident. In the

[32] Fletcher to Daniels, April 11, 1914 /11988.
[33] Miller, "Political Conditions."

clipped phraseology of official telegrams, omitting particles and other unessential words, he reported the arrest of the sailors, "part of whom were in boat with flag flying." The men were "marched" two blocks through the streets, he said, and then back to the boat. Although the federal commander had given an oral apology, "in view of publicity of event, I have called for formal disavowal and apology, and punishment of officer, and salute flag within 24 hours of 6 p.m. Thursday [April 9]."[34] This was all that Fletcher knew of the incident until Mayo made a fuller and more detailed report several days later. And since Fletcher forwarded Mayo's message to Washington exactly as he received it, it was almost all that Woodrow Wilson ever knew of the affair.

The crisis came at a particularly inopportune time for the American government. It was on a weekend, and President Wilson had left the capital to spend several days with his family in White Sulphur Springs, West Virginia. Fletcher got Mayo's message on Thursday night, April 9. By the time it had been encoded and sent to Key West, then to the Navy Department, decoded and relayed to Secretary of State Bryan, many hours had passed, and Wilson was already asleep in his hotel at the resort. Bryan was unwilling to act upon his own responsibility, however, and he sent on to the president the same skeletal account of the affair. In his telegram to Wilson he added the postscript: "I do not see that Mayo could have done otherwise. I await instructions."[35]

The occasion for Wilson's sojourn at White Sulphur Springs was the recurring illness—it was soon to prove fatal—of Mrs. Wilson. The president had hoped that a vacation away from the press of Washington's official and social

[34] Mayo to Fletcher, April 9, 1914, RG 45/659.
[35] Ray S. Baker, *Woodrow Wilson, Life and Letters* (Garden City, New York, 1927-1937), IV, 314; Bryan to Woodrow Wilson, April 10, 1914 /11633a.

activity might help her regain her waning strength. With
him and his wife were the Wilson daughters, their son-in-
law Francis B. Sayre, Secretary of the Treasury William G.
McAdoo (soon to marry Eleanor Wilson), and Dr. Cary
Grayson, the president's personal physician and favorite
golf partner. If Wilson was disturbed by the news from
Mexico, he did not indicate it to his family. On Friday he
played golf with Dr. Grayson and went for a buckboard
ride with Mrs. Wilson and their daughters. It was characteristic of the president that although McAdoo was a pros-
pective son-in-law and an important member of his cabinet,
he never mentioned the matter of the Tampico incident
while they were in White Sulphur Springs.[36]

By training and by occupation Woodrow Wilson should
have been a man to look at all sides of a question, weighing
evidence, seeking opinions and advice, before he made up
his mind. Snap judgments and obstinacy in maintaining
these judgments against all counter evidence are ordinarily not thought to be desirable traits in a dedicated
political scientist. More than that, Wilson's political philosophy was rooted in the enlightenment and drew sus-
tenance from the great liberals of the nineteenth century,
who saw their fellow human beings as rational creatures,
capable of settling almost any difficulty if only they would
use their reason. His ideal of a League of Nations, to be
born from the destruction of the Great War, was a monument to this deep conviction. Yet, combined with this
sincere and heartfelt confidence in man's reasonability,
was Wilson's almost perverse conviction that he, himself,
was perpetually right. He did not seek advice. Other men's
opinions did not really concern him, unless they should
happen to coincide with his. He was completely stubborn
about what he believed to be the correct course, and this,

[36] Ray S. Baker Papers, Library of Congress, Chronological File, Box
63, April 10, 1914; *Washington Post*, April 11, 1914, 1:3; *New York Times*,
April 12, 1914, 1:1.

perhaps, was the key to his success—as well as to his failures—as president of the United States.

Nothing bolsters a man's confidence in his own rectitude more than scanty information. To dissect an issue, to reflect, to question, to seek counsel—all of these serve only to confuse, to lead to doubt and uncertainty. Wilson had no need at White Sulphur Springs to consult McAdoo. He had made up his mind in the instant that he received Bryan's telegram, for by his unquestioning and unwavering support of Mayo's demands, Wilson achieved his aim of forcing a showdown with Victoriano Huerta. As a consequence, Wilson's policy in Mexico was constructed on sand, for neither he nor his secretary of state knew much of the events in Mexico during the next several days.

Whatever Woodrow Wilson's shortcomings, he was by no means a dishonest man. His failure to understand the situation in Mexico came not through a willful neglect of his duties as president, but through the self-deception that no more knowledge was required. Charles W. Thompson, a seasoned Washington reporter, wrote of the president: "Nobody who was competent to tell him the truth about Mexico could get his ear, could even get to his presence. It soon became a stock joke among the people who came to Washington, eager to lay their knowledge of Mexican conditions before him, that the only way to get to him was to tell Tumulty [the president's secretary] that you had never been in Mexico."[37]

A chief executive of the United States must rely in most circumstances upon cabinet members and upon their subordinates to supply information and advice. But Wilson's predilection for a strong presidency made this difficult, if not impossible. Thompson said of him: "Wilson never distrusted himself about anything, being more positive that

[37] Charles W. Thompson, *Presidents I've Known and Two Near Presidents* (Indianapolis, 1929), 261.

he was invariably right than any man I ever saw. It was simply his character to avoid expert authorities; he was acting according to his nature."[38] This was especially true in the field of foreign relations.

Although Wilson was the most highly educated man ever to become the president of the United States, his knowledge of foreign countries was narrowly limited. He remarked to a friend, as he entered the presidency, that it would be ironic if he were called upon to deal chiefly with foreign affairs.[39] Yet the exigencies of national Democratic politics had made it necessary for him to name as his secretary of state a man even less prepared for the task than he. William Jennings Bryan had engaged in politics for all of his adult life and had thrice essayed the presidential office, but his administrative abilities were slight, and his ken of public affairs was as restricted and parochial as his scientific horizon. The result of Bryan's inadequacies was that Woodrow Wilson became, for all intents, his own secretary of state. And since he made his own decisions without reference to the opinions of the American diplomats in Mexico, he was bound to make mistakes.

It was symptomatic of Wilson's lack of understanding of the events in Mexico that most of the career diplomats there either opposed his policies or gave him, at best, only halfhearted support. This was not solely, as Wilson suspected, because they owed their appointments to the previous Republican administration. In part this was true of the ambassador, Henry Lane Wilson. But even the subordinate officials were critical of the president, because they were on the scene and knew the situation as Woodrow Wilson could not. As Wilson had no confidence in his consuls, he came more and more to rely upon amateur diplomatists and special agents, responsible only to him or to Bryan. To

38 Thompson, *Presidents*, 261.
39 Baker, *Woodrow Wilson*, IV, 55.

Thompson they were a "curious and unfit lot. They appeared, as a rule, to be selected because they would give him
the side of the case that he had already decided to be the
right one, and the advice he had already given himself."[40]
Many of these agents did not speak Spanish and had never
been to Mexico. John Lind, the former governor of Minnesota, for example, knew nothing of the Mexican situation,
did not know the language, and was an implacable anti-
Catholic. He was singularly unequipped to handle his mission. Yet he had been sent to Mexico by Wilson and Bryan
to try to persuade Victoriano Huerta that he should resign
the presidency and hold free elections. Lind spent several
months in Mexico in a diplomatic limbo, because Huerta
would not receive him—since he had no diplomatic status—
and because Wilson would not acknowledge that the mission
had been a failure by ordering his recall.

On Friday, April 10, the president replied to Bryan's
telegram: "Mayo could not have done otherwise. O'Shaughnessy should be instructed to handle this matter with the
utmost earnestness, firmness and frankness, representing to
them its extreme seriousness and [the] possibility that
unless the guilty persons are promptly punished consequences of [the] gravest sort might ensue. . . . Lansing can,
of course, supply you with the precedents by which to
direct our course."[41] It is pertinent to note that Wilson
did not confine the issue to the situation at Tampico. Instead, the American protest would be carried directly to
Huerta's government in Mexico City. (As yet, Wilson could
not know that Morelos Zaragoza had also decided to refer
the matter to the Mexican Ministry of War.) The last
sentence in Wilson's telegram provides a clue to the president's real attitude, and this was to be his guide during the
coming days of negotiation: He did not request that Robert

40 Thompson, *Presidents*, 261-262.
41 Woodrow Wilson to Bryan, April 10, 1914 /11483.

Lansing (counselor of the State Department) find precedents to help shape his government's policies. Instead, Wilson wanted a rationalization for a predetermined course of action.

Having taken care of the problem most expeditiously and satisfactorily, the president went back to his golf and his family. He sent no more telegrams to Washington, nor was any news of the incident released by the State Department. The reporters in White Sulphur Springs and in Washington were given no inkling that a serious diplomatic crisis was brewing between the United States and Mexico, a crisis which might lead to hostilities between the two countries.

TWO

A Diplomatic Impasse

THE AMERICAN chargé d'affaires in Mexico City, Nelson J. O'Shaughnessy, was a man of elegant tastes. He had been born into a wealthy family—his father had been one of the chief promoters of the abortive Nicaraguan canal venture —and was educated at Oxford and at the Inner Temple in London. After taking the grand tour of the continent, polishing up his German and French, he received an appointment to the American Foreign Service in the administration of Theodore Roosevelt. Although he was virtually an expatriate, having spent most of his adult years abroad, O'Shaughnessy was closely identified with the Republican party. His interests were patrician. He and Mrs. O'Shaughnessy cultivated—almost curried—the friendship of the Roosevelts, the Vanderbilts, the Pattersons. In the cosmopolitan European society of the prewar years the O'Shaughnessys were intimates of princes, counts, and barons, of Russians, Hungarians, Austrians, Germans, and French. He began his diplomatic career at Copenhagen as a lowly third secretary, then moved to Berlin, and finally to Vienna, as second secretary of the embassy.

To the O'Shaughnessys, the ideal diplomatic life was a mad whirl of entertainment; gay parties and dances, bridge with important members of the local nobility, hunting roebuck in the Carpathians or perhaps in the Caucasus with Russian princes, and recouping one's health in Bohemia at the expensive and fashionable spas of Karlsbad and Marienbad. In Vienna, O'Shaughnessy would spend four or five hours at his desk and the rest of the day playing golf or at "the club." If he could—though the ambassador was not always agreeable—he would devote two months of the year to hunting expeditions. He spent money lavishly for clothes, ordering coats, waistcoats, trousers, and fancy smoking and hunting jackets from the most expensive and exclusive tailors in London. The O'Shaughnessys saw the temporary inconveniences of the minor posts only as necessary stepping stones in a successful diplomatic career, which would be culminated by an appointment as a minister or even an ambassador. And in this dream they were encouraged by the policies of the American Secretaries of State Elihu Root and Philander C. Knox in attracting to the Foreign Service wealthy young men who were highly educated, intelligent, and ambitious. The dream was shattered for the O'Shaughnessys, however, on the cruel rocks of economic exigencies. They simply could not afford to live on the money paid a young secretary of embassy. In Vienna, the rent alone on their fashionable apartment was higher than his year's salary.

Still, this would have been no problem had the elder O'Shaughnessy kept his fortune intact. He could have subsidized the young couple—and this was their intent—until they became self-sufficient in the diplomatic profession. But with the failure of the Nicaraguan canal scheme, O'Shaughnessy's father lost virtually all of his fortune. His attempt to make a financial comeback by promoting a new mechanical device for picking cotton also failed, in part because the machine would not work, but perhaps chiefly because the panic of 1907 prevented him from selling shares in the company even to a gullible American public. At a time, then, when the young couple was most dependent upon him for assistance, the elder O'Shaughnessy could offer them nothing but hopes for affluence in the future. In the end, the O'Shaughnessys borrowed, cadged, and wheedled money from banks and from friends in many countries, giving in return notes payable by the father, who was himself struggling to keep his nose above the waters of a financial maelstrom. The result was that Nelson and Edith O'Shaughnessy lived for several years in Vienna in genteel penury, evading or stalling creditors, grasping for straws in the hope that his father would achieve a sudden and dramatic return to wealth.

Just when the situation seemed most dire, O'Shaughnessy was moved to Mexico City. He fought the transfer to the last, for all his ties were to European society, and Mexico seemed beyond the pale of civilization. But in Mexico City his situation began to improve. He worked harder than he ever had in his life. Relations between the United States and the Austro-Hungarian empire had been quite unimportant. In Mexico there was now more to do in a day in the embassy than in several weeks at Vienna. And when the ambassador, Henry Lane Wilson, was withdrawn in the summer of 1913, in part because he was a Republican who disagreed with the administration's policies, but also as a sign of the displeasure of President Wilson with Huerta, O'Shaughnessy's star seemed in the ascendant. He was now made chargé d'affaires, and he and Mrs. O'Shaughnessy lived in the embassy. His salary was considerably higher. If he still owed debts in Europe, if their family furniture was held in storage in Vienna tied up by a court action of one of his creditors, nevertheless, for the first time since their marriage they could feel economically comfortable. And above all, as the representative of the United States, O'Shaughnessy was the most important diplomat in Mexico. He was a particularly close friend of the Mexican president.

From the beginning, Huerta took pains to flatter the O'Shaughnessys. He called O'Shaughnessy "son" and conferred *abrazos* (the bearhugs and backslapping by which Mexicans attest masculine esteem) upon him. The president made a practice of taking Edith O'Shaughnessy's arm as they entered salons where state dinners or receptions were held. Their sudden diplomatic eminence and the attentions of the president pleased the O'Shaughnessys, the more so since their position in Mexico City contrasted so strongly with the vexations of life in Vienna. They were genuinely fond of Huerta and recognized his abilities. They were not blind to his faults, above all, his drinking, but they also realized that Madero, whatever his idealism, could not give Mexico a strong government. O'Shaughnessy was not publicly critical of the American president, nor did he follow the course begun by Ambassador Wilson of urging that the American government grant recognition to Huerta. But he did use his close friendship with the Mexican president to settle problems smoothly.

Although Huerta refused to heed Wilson's demands that he resign and hold free elections in Mexico, he was amiable in many small ways toward the United States and its young representative. Regardless of President Wilson's attitude toward Huerta, there was little cause for complaint about the treatment of American nationals or their property in those areas dominated by the federal armies. Most of the destruction of American property and the incidents involving American citizens came about because of the revolution against Huerta. Nevertheless, Wilson had hardened his heart against the Mexican president and held him responsible, not only for the death of Madero, but the continued unrest, rapine, and disorder in Mexico. Since Wilson's magic panacea for Mexico was an end to the revolution and the holding of free elections, and these could be accomplished only by the elimination of Victoriano Huerta, in a sense, the American president and his chargé d'affaires in Mexico City were working at cross-purposes. O'Shaughnessy followed the instructions from Washington scrupulously and loyally, but he believed, nonetheless, that they were asinine.[1]

The first news of the Tampico incident reached O'Shaughnessy from the Mexican foreign office, not from Washington. And for several days he was handicapped in his negotiations with Huerta's government by not having a copy of Mayo's ultimatum, much less a complete knowledge of what had happened at Tampico. On the morning of April 10, at the fashionable Jockey Club, he received a note from Roberto A. Esteva Ruiz, the Mexican under secretary of foreign relations, informing him that a group of "marines" had been arrested near the Iturbide Bridge in Tampico. General Morelos Zaragoza had taken prompt action, said Esteva Ruiz, in ordering their release and the arrest of Colonel Hinojosa. He said that the incident was inconsequential and compared the action of the federal commander to similar cases in the American Civil War, when ports had been closed to all outsiders. He said that the arrest was understandable, if not justifiable, and asked, in view of the verbal apology of Morelos Zaragoza, that the demands of Mayo be withdrawn. O'Shaughnessy was puzzled as to what these demands might be and what course of action he was expected to follow. It was not until much later in the afternoon that he got from Fletcher an outline of the events—as seen from the American point

[1] Nelson J. and Edith O'Shaughnessy Papers, New York Public Library; State Department Files, National Archives, 123, Os4. The material on the O'Shaughnessys in this chapter and elsewhere in the book are drawn from these extensive collections.

of view—and a copy of Mayo's ultimatum. Bypassing the Ministry of Foreign Relations, O'Shaughnessy hurried to find Huerta to obtain the president's personal intervention in the matter. He still had heard no word from his own department.[2]

To find the president of Mexico was no mean feat, for Huerta rarely came to the presidential palace. Instead, he spent much of the day in his automobile, going from one military function to another, and his evenings and nights at disreputable restaurants or in saloons. Huerta was always a heavy drinker, but now, after a discouraging year in the presidency, he drank copiously and almost continuously. Whenever O'Shaughnessy wished to take up some official matter with Huerta, he was forced to drive about the city from place to place until he could locate the president and his party. Esteva Ruiz went with O'Shaughnessy to represent the Ministry of Foreign Relations. Although he was in charge of Mexico's diplomatic affairs (since the secretary, José López Portillo y Rojas, was ill and had gone to a resort on Lake Chapala to regain his health), Esteva Ruiz had not met Huerta before. In fact, Huerta had never even heard of his minister, and it was necessary for O'Shaughnessy to introduce the two Mexicans when they finally tracked down the president. At O'Shaughnessy's request, Huerta gave him a written statement which paralleled that of Esteva Ruiz, and he too asked the United States to retire the ultimatum of Mayo. Huerta added a few oral observations on the incident. These, according to Mrs. O'Shaughnessy, were "beyond editing." Whatever they were, they were not reported to the State Department.[3]

O'Shaughnessy had the notes of Huerta and Esteva Ruiz

[2] Edith O'Shaughnessy, *A Diplomat's Wife in Mexico* (New York, 1916), 258; R. A. Esteva Ruiz to O'Shaughnessy, April 10, 1914 /11659; *La Patria*, April 21, 1914, 1:4-5.

[3] From a personal conversation with Esteva Ruiz in the summer of 1958; O'Shaughnessy, *Diplomat's Wife*, 258.

translated, and he released them to the American reporters in the Mexican capital. It was for this reason that the first accounts in American newspapers came from the Associated Press in Mexico City and not from Washington.[4] (Huerta's tight censorship kept all mention of the incident from the Mexican newspapers for several days.) There were two errors in the story of the Associated Press, one perhaps owing to O'Shaughnessy's faulty Spanish, the other to his vivid imagination. The first was to identify the arrested seamen as "marines," a possible mistranslation of the Spanish "marineros." The error was of little importance, but it was symptomatic of the chronic lack of exact information in Washington that most of the members of the American government, including the president and the secretary of state, thought for several days that the men were marines.

The second error, though at first glance minor, proved to be important in the long run. Where dispatches from the American naval officers reported that the arrested sailors had been "marched" through the streets, O'Shaughnessy made it "paraded," and all newspaper accounts in the United States used that term. "Marched" is a neutral word. "Paraded," on the other hand, signified that the insult to American honor had been flamboyant and flagrant. It helped Americans inside and outside the government to feel that Mayo was completely justified in demanding a severe penalty from the Mexicans in Tampico. It also made it easier for the United States to feel put upon and to insist that Mayo's demands be followed to the letter.

Yet, if honor was important to the United States, it was doubly so to Mexico. A great country can afford to be magnanimous, for it loses none of its strength through its magnanimity. When a nation is weak, national honor and pride are of the utmost importance. To be weak and

[4] *New York Times*, April 11, 1914, 1:1; *New York World*, April 11, 1914, 1:1.

humbled as well is too much for the national spirit to bear. Mexico's military record was unimpressive. She had won no wars, and all of her military heroes were those who had given their lives in a lost cause. Mexico has more national holidays than the United States, and the Mexicans celebrate these joyfully with ringing oratory extolling the *patria,* with elaborate fireworks displays, and with fine parades. Pride in country was a great thing to the Mexicans. It was difficult enough for the United States to retreat from its stand, but for Mexico it was well-nigh impossible. To prevent hostilities between the two countries, some spirit of compromise would be necessary. Unfortunately, neither Wilson nor Huerta was in a conciliatory mood.

To Huerta an appeal to national honor and patriotism seemed his last chance to keep the presidency. With the rebel armies in Torreón and bearing down on Zacatecas, he could no longer hope to win against the Constitutionalists by military action. It was a desperate gamble, but it was barely possible that the threat of American intervention might bring unity to the contending factions. If he could defy the United States and uphold Mexican honor, his people might turn to him as their national leader. Even the revolutionaries might prefer him to the foreign invaders. Since he had nothing to lose, Huerta could afford to be adamant about the salute. Not once in the days that followed did he withdraw from this first stand; he would not admit that the Mexicans were the offenders at Tampico.

On the evening of April 10, O'Shaughnessy still had heard nothing from Washington. He cabled Bryan that, on the basis of the information he then possessed, he had made "representations" to Huerta. The Mexican president, he said, had promised an investigation of the incident but brushed it off as "nothing more than the misunderstanding of a subordinate official" who had been punished by his superior. The consul in Tampico, Clarence Miller, had been unable to express his disagreement with the actions of Mayo, but O'Shaughnessy was less inhibited. He told Bryan frankly: "I do not quite understand such an ultimatum being issued without superior authority, in view of the tense situation now existing." He could not know that Wilson had already decided to support Mayo without reservation.[5]

It was not until the following morning that Bryan's first message concerning the incident reached the American embassy in Mexico City. Because the secretary of state knew little of what had happened at Tampico, he was unable to give O'Shaughnessy more information than he already had. Bryan stressed the seriousness of the situation, however, and asked that the guilty parties be "promptly punished." He did not mention Mayo's demand for a salute. Since Wilson was still in White Sulphur Springs, Bryan had to await his return before he could take more definitive action.[6]

In Washington, Bryan had now received O'Shaughnessy's cablegram, and he was immediately cheered by what he thought to be Huerta's promptness in apologizing. Bryan was the eternal optimist, and he often read into the dispatches from Mexico much that was not there. In his statements to American reporters, who had come to the State Department to inquire about the Associated Press article from Mexico City, he exuded confidence. "I am inclined to believe," he said, "that Admiral Mayo, who after all has this whole matter in his hands, will regard the apology as sufficient. The greater includes the less, and if the federal commander at Tampico should not actually salute the flag, Admiral Mayo will pass by the matter, satisfied with what Huerta has said of the incident."[7] If Bryan be-

---

[5] O'Shaughnessy to Bryan, April 10, 1914 /11484.
[6] Bryan to O'Shaughnessy, April 10, 1914 /11483.
[7] *New York Times*, April 12, 1914, 3:2.

lieved this, however, he had seriously misjudged the temper of the United States president and navy. In the meantime, Wilson remained in seclusion in White Sulphur Springs, refusing to make a statement to the press. He had come to rest, he said, and did not intend to discuss any official business. Instead, he played golf again with Dr. Grayson and enjoyed, while he could, this brief vacation with his family.[8]

Had Bryan exercised more leadership in molding foreign affairs, he might have made a compromise possible, for the matter of a military salute was of little importance to him. He was more than willing to accept the implied apologies of the Mexican government. Bryan could not face the harsh fact that the consequences of a strong stand at Tampico might be armed intervention. He saw the danger of war and was therefore unable to act decisively. Wilson was of a different stripe; he acted with decision by ignoring the consequences. In his failure to take command of the situation, to make known his views to the president, the secretary of state abdicated the high responsibilities of his office in favor of the more militant opinions of the navy and of Wilson. Instead of sending directives to Mayo, Bryan vacillated, waiting to see what Mayo would do at Tampico. Nor was the admiral inclined to lessen his demands. Having received no deterring words from Washington, he stationed *Des Moines* close to the shore at Arbol Grande with her decks ostentatiously cleared for action. Mayo told Fletcher that he thought "the moral effect would be beneficial."[9]

By the weekend, O'Shaughnessy was experiencing considerable difficulty in locating officials of the Mexican government to whom he could deliver Bryan's dispatches. It was the beginning of Holy Week, when public life in Mexico grinds to a halt and almost every functionary takes a vaca-

[8] *Washington Post*, April 12, 1914, 1:3; Baker Chronological File, Box 63, April 10, 1914.
[9] Mayo to Fletcher, April 11, 1914, RG 45/659.

tion. Not even an impending international crisis could halt the exodus of government employees from the capital. When O'Shaughnessy informed him of this, Bryan was pleased to extend Mayo's deadline for compliance with the American demands. Thereafter, Bryan's spirits soared and plummeted like a barometer in obedience to the tidings from Mexico.[10]

The first clear-cut statement defining the position of the Mexican government came on April 12. In the morning, O'Shaughnessy paid a call at Foreign Relations and had the good fortune to find Esteva Ruiz still in his office. The under secretary said once more that Huerta could not accede to the demands of the United States, that the president considered the apology of Morelos Zaragoza and the subsequent arrest of Hinojosa sufficient reparation. O'Shaughnessy replied that his government would not accept a verbal refusal. He asked that Huerta reconsider his position. He warned Esteva Ruiz that Huerta's attitude was "fraught with the most serious possibilities," for the American people might force their president "to uphold our national dignity, even with armed force, if necessary." In the afternoon, Esteva Ruiz delivered a note to the embassy in which his government again refused to bow to the American demand. He contended that the "marines" had landed at a place where there were military operations and without previous permission from the federal authorities. It was understandable, he said, that Hinojosa should believe himself authorized to arrest them. His government felt that Morelos Zaragoza had given the Americans "ample satisfaction." The under secretary added that Huerta had directed him to say that his government would not apologize or salute the American flag, for "carrying courtesy to that point would be equivalent to accepting the sovereignty

[10] O'Shaughnessy to Bryan, April 11, 1914 /11487; Bryan to O'Shaughnessy, April 11, 1914 /11487.

of a foreign state to the derogation of national dignity and decorum, which the president is disposed to have respected in any case."[11]

O'Shaughnessy told Esteva Ruiz that he regarded Huerta's attitude as "ill advised," and said that the Mexican government must reconsider its position. The under secretary answered that Huerta feared there would be serious anti-American outbreaks throughout Mexico if he submitted to the "humiliating terms of the United States." When O'Shaughnessy relayed Huerta's note to Washington, its bleakness disappointed Bryan, who had been prepared for more hopeful news. He replied that he could not give an answer until President Wilson returned from White Sulphur Springs.[12]

In the past, O'Shaughnessy had been able to gain his way with Huerta by appealing to their personal friendship. He hoped now to conceive some stratagem to bring the crisis to a happy solution. But he was vexed by the hours wasted in pursuit of the elusive president, and he decided that the next overtures must be made by Huerta. That afternoon, however, as he and Mrs. O'Shaughnessy were passing the Chapultepec Restaurant, they noticed the presidential car parked in front. O'Shaughnessy strolled casually through the restaurant, to give Huerta an opportunity to call him over to his table if he wished. Huerta was dining with a military group and did not see his friend, and since the American chargé d'affaires would not give the appearance that he was seeking out the president, the ruse was unsuccessful. In any event, there could be no further overtures toward the Mexican government until Wilson was again in Washington.[13]

Since it now appeared that Huerta would not agree to

[11] O'Shaughnessy to Bryan, April 12, 1914 /11485; O'Shaughnessy to Bryan, April 12, 1914 /11486; O'Shaughnessy, *Diplomat's Wife*, 260-261.
[12] Bryan to O'Shaughnessy, April 12, 1914 /11486.
[13] O'Shaughnessy, *Diplomat's Wife*, 261.

salute the American flag, the navy began to make preparations for military action at Tampico. Josephus Daniels asked Fletcher if Mayo had sufficient force under his command to seize and hold the city. This was the first indication of what Washington intended to do if the Mexicans should remain adamant. Both Mayo and Fletcher expressed their optimism about the success of a landing; aboard *Dolphin,* Mayo and his senior officers, in anticipation that their men would soon go ashore at Tampico, drew up their battle plans. The smaller vessels would continue to operate inside the river; *Dolphin* would seize the customhouse and fiscal wharf; *Chester* and *Des Moines* would capture or sink the Mexican gunboats. The two battleships and *San Francisco* would anchor as close to the bar as possible to permit the easy discharge of their ship's companies.[14]

What at first had appeared to be a comparatively simple and safe maneuver took on a more formidable aspect as the actual plans were made. Several difficulties presented themselves to Mayo and his officers. The first of these was the shallow bar. Since none of the larger vessels could cross it, small boats would be required to shuttle the men into Tampico from outside the river. This operation would be hazardous if the landing were opposed. Though there was a broad beach at La Barra where a landing could be effected from the open sea, the American boats would be forced to ground on a sand ridge one hundred yards out, while the men struggled ashore through waist-deep, shark-infested water. And the wooded sandhills behind the beach made excellent cover for the defenders. Unless the guns of the battleships laid down a cruel barrage on the Mexican lines, the Americans could suffer heavy casualties. Moreover,

[14] Daniels to Fletcher, April 12, 1914 /11988; Fletcher to Daniels, April 12, 1914 /11988; Mayo, "Campaign Order No. 1," April 12, 1914, RG 45/659.

there was the possibility that the Constitutionalists at Tampico would join forces with the federals to repel the foreign invaders. Since Morelos Zaragoza had close to three thousand troops under his command (admittedly of poor quality), and the rebels could count on nearly that number, Mayo might well find his task difficult. And to complicate the matter further, any "norther" would make it impossible to cross the bar in either direction for two or three days at a stretch.[15]

As a landing in force became less attractive, Mayo explored the possibility of shelling the city if the salute were not fired. He soon found that this could not be permitted, for Tampico had no shore defenses, and international law banned the shelling of unfortified cities. As the week wore on, and as the naval commanders debated what punishment to inflict upon Huerta, Tampico seemed less and less attractive as a site for the retaliation. Blood would be shed and American honor might be vindicated by an attack at Tampico, but Huerta would not be weakened in any way.

Although Mayo had been highly optimistic on the twelfth about the success of a landing, by the following day he was less certain. As he had anticipated, a "norther" blew up, and he was afraid that a sudden worsening of the crisis might find his small vessels trapped inside the river, with the battleships outside unable to give any assistance. He and his staff had reached the reluctant conclusion that there was now not sufficient force within the river—given the many obstacles—to take Tampico. As a consequence, Mayo decided to withdraw all of his ships from the river until the issue could be resolved between Washington and Mexico City. This action, if the Constitutionalists should renew their attack, would leave a large number of Americans helpless in Tampico. Mayo therefore informed Clar-

---

[15] War Portfolio No. 1, Information Section (Mexico), GBR.

ence Miller that he would take aboard his ships all those who wished to go outside the bar.[16]

The publication of this notice by Miller led most Americans in Tampico to believe that the navy contemplated immediate military action, perhaps a bombardment of the city, and several hundred men, women, and children flocked to the wharves to seek refuge on the cruisers. But in the midst of the evacuation, Mayo changed his mind. He had received word from Washington (Bryan's reaction to the first note of O'Shaughnessy) which seemed to indicate a lessening of the crisis, and he concluded that hostilities were not now imminent. Moreover, Admiral Fletcher and his superiors in the Navy Department strongly disapproved of his withdrawing *Dolphin* and the cruisers from the river. The refugees coming to the dock were asked to return to their homes, while those on the cruisers and those already taken out to the battleships were landed once more. Completely oblivious of the problems of diplomats and naval commanders, the Americans in Tampico could only be apprehensive about Mayo's seeming indecision. From their viewpoint it seemed that neither the navy nor the United States government had any real interest in their lives or properties. And in this they were at least partly right; they were the dispensable pawns in the greater game of the destruction of Huerta's regime.[17]

Wilson returned to Washington from White Sulphur Springs on Monday morning, April 13. Mrs. Wilson remained at the resort during the week which followed in the hope that more rest might speed her convalescence. The president brought with him the determination, born in the first hours of the Tampico crisis, not to yield an inch to the Huerta government. He was in a bellicose mood as he told

16 Mayo to Fletcher, April 13, 1914 /11988; Mayo to Miller, April 13, 1914, PRT 800/682; Miller to Mayo, April 13, 1914, RG 45/659.

17 Mayo to Fletcher, April 14, 1914, RG 45/659; Miller, "Political Conditions."

reporters who met his train: "The salute will be fired." The dispatches from O'Shaughnessy, which had accumulated on his desk over the weekend, only served to strengthen Wilson's inflexibility, for it seemed to him that Huerta took the incident much too lightly. He prepared personally a strongly worded statement for Bryan to send to O'Shaughnessy, insisting upon full compliance with the demands of the United States. Having taken care of the diplomatic situation, the president accompanied Dr. Grayson to the country club for an afternoon round of golf.[18]

By coincidence, John Lind arrived in Washington at the same time as the president. After seven fruitless, uncomfortable months in Mexico, he was returning to the United States, ostensibly for reasons of health. His return was, nonetheless, an admission by the American government that Huerta could not be removed solely by diplomatic negotiations. Lind had already left Veracruz when the Tampico incident occurred. His arrival in Washington was singularly opportune for Wilson, because he told the president what he wanted to hear—the United States must take a strong position with Huerta.

At 10 a.m. on April 14, Lind and Bryan came to the White House to confer with the president on the situation in Mexico. Lind emphasized that Wilson's policy of "watchful waiting" had not effected any change. Although the hostile attitude of the United States and Wilson's refusal to grant recognition to Huerta had been meant to weaken the Mexican government, Huerta had nevertheless continued to receive funds and arms, said Lind. And he was in the process of negotiating another loan with French bankers to be secured by the port revenues of Veracruz. Despite the defeat of the federal army at Torreón, Lind thought that Huerta would now be able to hold out indefinitely.

[18] *New York World*, April 14, 1914, 1:1; Baker Chronological File, Box 63, April 13, 1914.

He told Wilson that the United States should stand firm in its demands and should not make any compromise with Huerta.[19]

An hour later the president met with his cabinet to lay out the course to be pursued with Mexico. The meeting was more an instruction than a discussion. After hearing the facts of the incident, as sketched by Wilson, the cabinet members were unanimous in their opinion that Huerta must be forced to comply with Mayo's ultimatum. Only Secretary Bryan seemed disturbed by the possible consequences, but he did not oppose Wilson. McAdoo stood most strongly for intervention. He said that if it were necessary for the United States to send troops into Mexico, they should be kept there indefinitely. At the close of the short meeting, Wilson advised the secretaries that if they believed in the efficacy of prayer, he hoped they would pray for peace. He gave no hint of the momentous decision he would make later that day.[20]

Robert Lansing had been working over the weekend, diligently searching through the department's archives for some earlier incident upon which to base the American case. On the fourteenth he reported his findings to the president. It had been necessary to go back more than sixty years, but Lansing found a precedent, as Wilson had been certain he would. In 1854, he said, American ships shelled Greytown (San Juan del Norte), Nicaragua, in retaliation for an alleged insult to the consul stationed at that city. With ample precedent in hand, Wilson's position now wore an air of legality and respectability—at least in his own mind. More important than the ferreting out of the Greytown affair, from Wilson's point of view, was Lansing's opinion that the constitutional delegation to Congress of the power

19 Baker Chronological File, Box 63, April 14, 1914; George M. Stephenson, *John Lind of Minnesota* (Minneapolis, 1935), 263-264.
20 House Diary, April 15, 1914, Edward House Papers, Yale University.

to make war did not preclude the use of force by the president to enforce demands or to make reprisals. Wilson now decided upon a spectacular demonstration of American armed might in an attempt to intimidate Huerta's government. On the afternoon of the fourteenth—though he had not mentioned the matter to his cabinet earlier the same day—he ordered the Atlantic Fleet to Mexican waters to reinforce the ships under the command of Mayo and Fletcher.[21]

At the same time that Wilson was conferring with Lind and with his cabinet, O'Shaughnessy in Mexico City was running down the elusive Huerta to deliver the latest American note. They had not met for four days, but O'Shaughnessy found Huerta even more obstinate than before. In all, he spent two hours with the Mexican president, part of the time in Huerta's private automobile, the rest—with Edith O'Shaughnessy—at a review of Huerta's mounted police. This was an official function, but the O'Shaughnessys were the only foreigners to be invited to the parade. Whatever the trouble between their two governments, the personal relationship between Huerta and the young Americans remained unchanged. According to the correspondent for the *Washington Post*, they chatted and joked "in a very cordial fashion." When the chargé d'affaires returned to his embassy to file a dispatch to Secretary Bryan, Mrs. O'Shaughnessy remained with Huerta for an "elaborate collation" of champagne, cold *patés*, and sweetmeats. She was seated in the place of honor, at the president's right.[22]

O'Shaughnessy reported his conversation with Huerta

[21] Robert Lansing, "Memorandum," April 14, 1914 /11510½; Ivon D. Spencer, *The Victor and the Spoils* (Providence, 1959), 309-317; *New York Times*, April 15, 1914, 1:8; *New York World*, April 15, 1914, 1:7-8; 2:1-2; "Miscellaneous Memorandum," April 14, 1914, Secretary of the Navy Papers, National Archives.

[22] O'Shaughnessy to Bryan, April 14, 1914 /11514; *Washington Post*, April 16, 1914, 1:3; O'Shaughnessy, *Diplomat's Wife*, 263.

to Bryan, adding: "As usual with me, he was very com-
municative and most familiar." The young diplomat was
increasingly self-satisfied, for in these days there was no
more important American diplomatic post in the world.
The many years of scrimping on the insignificant salary of a
third or second secretary, of incurring bad debts, of avoiding
one's friends to whom one owed money, seemed far behind now. O'Shaughnessy yearned to bring off some great
coup to demonstrate his usefulness to the State Department.
Already he could savor the fruits of his reward—he would
become a minister or an ambassador in a great European
country. But it was a vain dream. Though he did not realize
it, he was merely digging deeper his own diplomatic grave.
When he stressed his close friendship with Huerta in his
dispatches to the department as evidence of his indispensa-
bility, Wilson saw only a confirmation of his belief that old-
line diplomats, and O'Shaughnessy in particular, were not
to be trusted. And the opposition newspapers in the United
States, especially the *Washington Post*, the *New York Sun*,
and the *Herald*, added fuel to the fires of Wilson's anger,
whenever they could, by pointing up each instance of in-
timacy with the Mexican president. It was most unfair
to O'Shaughnessy, because for almost the first time in his
life he was doing a thoroughly competent and conscien-
tious job.

In his long interview with the Mexican president,
O'Shaughnessy pointed out the "regrettable results" of
Huerta's intransigence. Huerta countered that Hinojosa's
arrest of the sailors was the result of ignorance, not of ani-
mosity, and that this should extenuate the act. He said that
the American government should accept Morelos Zaragoza's
voluntary expression of regret, especially since the United
States was dealing with a weaker nation, torn by revolution, and with a regime which was "struggling to uphold
the dignity and sovereignty of Mexico." Huerta thought

the matter might be resolved by placing the case before the
Hague tribunal. O'Shaughnessy wrote to Bryan: "The old
Indian was more eloquent than I have ever seen him, and
I was impressed that he is imbued with a certain amount
of patriotism in his statements, and I believe that he will
probably not yield."[23]

It was clear to O'Shaughnessy that Huerta welcomed the
thought of American intervention, that only by this means
could his government be saved. Later the same day this
view was substantiated by Huerta himself. When he was
informed by a reporter that Wilson had ordered a great
fleet to Mexican waters, the president exclaimed: "Is it a
calamity? No. It is the best thing that could happen to us."[24]

Even as Huerta spoke, ships from several American ports
converged upon Mexico. There were seven of the newest
and most powerful battleships, four troop transports with
their full contingents of marines, several cruisers, and a
destroyer flotilla, all under the command of Vice Admiral
Charles T. Badger. It was a formidable array of modern
seapower.

It is uncertain what Wilson hoped to accomplish by this
action. Ostensibly he would force the Mexicans to salute
the American flag, to acknowledge that American honor
had been sullied at Tampico. If no salute was forthcoming,
these ships would be used in some as yet undetermined way
to punish the culprits. Yet the conclusion is unavoidable
that not even a sudden capitulation by Huerta on the matter
of the salute would have stayed the Atlantic Fleet. Nor
would Wilson have been satisfied. He now professed to see
a pattern of "studied contempt" toward the United States
on the part of the Mexican government. On April 15 Wilson prepared a statement for the press (and for Huerta
as well) in which he emphasized the fact that the Tampico

[23] O'Shaughnessy to Bryan, April 14, 1914 /11514.
[24] O'Shaughnessy, *Diplomat's Wife*, 266.

incident "must not be thought of alone." There had been "many cases," he said, "of the flouting of the rights of American citizens or the dignity of the government of the United States, and no attempt at either reparation or correction." He cited the incident at Veracruz when a naval mail orderly had been "arrested and put into jail," and, "most serious of all," the withholding of "an official dispatch of the government of the United States" in Mexico City. It was significant, Wilson said, that similar incidents did not occur with regard to other nationalities or other governments.[25]

It was true that these two incidents had taken place. But it was equally true that Wilson exaggerated their seriousness. He saw in each instance precisely what he wanted to see—mounting evidence of the anti-American attitude of Huerta's government. No incident was too trivial to be seized upon and magnified—or even distorted—for Wilson must have known, whatever he might say to the contrary in public, that the arrest of the sailors alone was indeed a flimsy excuse for military intervention. Thus the two new incidents assumed a meaning far beyond their intrinsic importance.

During the night of April 10 the battleship *Minnesota* had come down from Tampico to Veracruz to be coaled. Early the next morning, a seaman, F. C. Larue, came ashore to pick up the mail for Mayo's division. As he was leaving the post office, Larue was manhandled by a federal soldier. The Mexican had evidently confused Larue with a marine deserter whose photograph was on the post office wall and for whose apprehension a reward had been offered. Since neither could understand the other's language, a policeman took both to the police station, where there was an interpreter. The matter was cleared up within a short time, and Larue was permitted to return to his ship. The affair was

[25] *New York Times,* April 16, 1914, 1:6-7; Bryan to O'Shaughnessy, April 15, 1914 /11519.

considered by the captain to be so insignificant that it was not even noted in the ship's log.[26]

William W. Canada, the American consul in Veracruz, learned of the incident, however, and cabled a garbled version to the State Department. According to Canada, Larue had been "arrested by a policeman . . . and taken to the jail."[27] But the plain fact was that Larue was taken *to* the jail only in the sense that it and the police station were one and the same thing. A dispatch to the *New York Herald*, printed on April 12, put the matter in its true light. Fletcher, after a thorough investigation—and at a time when the navy would have welcomed another incident to prove that the Huerta regime was capable of any number of hostile acts against the Americans—told Secretary Daniels: "The attitude of the Mexican authorities was correct; there is no cause for complaint against them, and the incident is without significance."[28]

In making an issue of this supposed arrest, Wilson demonstrated conclusively that he did not know what was happening in Mexico. He was completely unaware of the story in the *Herald*, which had appeared three days earlier (it was, after all, an opposition newspaper), and he did not see the dispatches from Fletcher, which proved Canada's account to be erroneous. Worst of all, Wilson misread what little evidence he did have. He said that the orderly had been "put into jail," which Canada had never said. And he referred to the "nominal punishment" inflicted on the "officer" who arrested him, and asserted that Larue had been "picked out" from the many persons "constantly . . . going ashore on various errands from the various warships in the harbor, representing several nations."[29]

---

[26] *New York Herald*, April 12, 1914, 1:1-2; *Minnesota* Log, April 11, 1914; Fletcher to Daniels, April 16, 1914 /11559.
[27] Canada to Bryan, April 12, 1914 /11478.
[28] Fletcher to Daniels, April 16, 1914 /11559.
[29] Bryan to O'Shaughnessy, April 15, 1914 /11519.

Nor was the third incident more grave than the first two. Because of the crisis in his relations with the United States, as well as the recent victories of the rebels in the North, Huerta's government had instituted a severe censorship on all cable and telegraph lines connecting the Mexican capital with the outside world. Huerta was determined that no word of either of these crises appear in the Mexican newspapers or reach his people. All messages were checked by a censor, and any person who sent or received communications in code was required to bring a key to the telegraph office to have them decoded. Diplomatic messages were, of course, exempted from the censorship. Late on the evening of April 11 an employee in the censor's office quite innocently and ignorantly held up a coded cablegram from Bryan to the American embassy. When O'Shaughnessy had not received a reply for several hours to dispatches he had sent to Bryan earlier in the day, he called the telegraph office and learned for the first time of the delayed message from Washington. According to Mrs. O'Shaughnessy, the matter was cleared up in two minutes. "It was less than nothing," she wrote her mother. O'Shaughnessy reported the incident to Bryan in his next dispatch, but minimized its importance. In all, the cablegram was held up 55 minutes.[30]

The secretary of state had already heard about the delay from a different source. The superintendent of the Mexican Telegraph Company in Mexico City reported the incident to his superiors, who relayed the information to Washington. The telegraph official corroborated O'Shaughnessy's opinion that the detention had not been deliberate, but was "due to a misunderstanding of duty by the censor." He added that there had been no further trouble with dispatches. Bryan, since he had not at that time received O'Shaughnessy's report of the incident, ordered O'Shaughnessy to

[30] *El Imparcial*, April 12, 1914, 1:1; O'Shaughnessy, *Diplomat's Wife*, 269.

investigate immediately and to demand the message. In his reply to Bryan, O'Shaughnessy magnified his efforts somewhat, asserting that he had made "robust representations." He emphasized again that the "non-delivery was really due to the ignorance of the censor."[31] This would have ended the matter had it not been for Wilson's determination to build his case on the supposed hostility of Huerta's government toward the United States. And once again he did not seek to ascertain the facts before he made his charges.

On the morning of April 15, President Wilson summoned ranking members of the two foreign relations committees of Congress to the White House to explain the administration's position. He did not solicit their advice or counsel. He was convinced, he told the legislators, that there would be no salute. He recited the three incidents which had caused him to dispatch the fleet to Mexico. Admitting that they might seem "slight in themselves," Wilson insisted that they were of extreme importance when considered in connection with the "general conduct" of the Mexican government toward the United States and its citizens. The president found complete bipartisan support; among the Democrats, if for no other reason than party loyalty; among the Republicans, because they believed he should have taken a strong position regarding Mexico many months earlier.

Wilson outlined to the legislators the tentative plans of his government, which might include, he said, the seizure of Veracruz and Tampico and other ports on both coasts and perhaps a peaceful blockade of Mexico. The occupation of these ports would cease, he added, when American honor had been "satisfied." He indicated that there was

[31] *New York Times,* April 17, 1914, 2:7-8; Bryan to O'Shaughnessy, April 12, 1914, State Department Files, 119.23/a; O'Shaughnessy to Bryan, April 12, 1914, State Department Files, 119.23/1.

ample precedent for carrying out these actions by presidential order, but he and the legislators agreed that since Congress was in session, it would be better to seek support in both houses through the joint resolution. None of the senators or representatives, whether Democratic or Republican, felt that there would be any difficulty in securing the approval of Congress.[32]

There was, in fact, little opposition in the United States to Wilson's proposed course of action. Many, perhaps most, Americans, who knew even less concerning the events in Mexico than did their president, felt that American honor must be restored, that Huerta must be brought to salute the flag, by armed force, if necessary. The popular response in the United States was largely emotional. It was an era of national naivete in which the spirit of patriotism was waxing, in which people could be stirred to action by magical words about the *Maine*, Cuba, or the Philippines, and in which foreigners, especially Filipinos or Latin Americans, were thought to be inferior to Americans. It was easy for the president to capitalize on these national emotions, and had he decided to occupy large parts of Mexican territory, he would have found the country largely with him. Those who opposed Wilson were, in the main, from church groups (though not the larger denominations) and the more radical labor unions. William Haywood of the International Workers of the World threatened a general strike if United States forces should move into Mexico. But the I.W.W. was having sufficient difficulty of its own—the coal strike in Colorado was being smashed with the aid of state troopers—without essaying a nationwide strike. Although Wilson received many letters of protest, they did not come from responsible organizations or important persons. The United States could have gone to war against Mexico, and the

[32] *New York Times*, April 16, 1914, 1:1; 2:1; *New York World*, April 16, 1914, 1:7-8.

people would have flocked to the colors. The newspapers of the country, both administration and opposition, gave the president their warm and wholehearted support.[33]

In Mexico City, O'Shaughnessy continued his efforts to persuade President Huerta to agree to the American demands. He knew the wily old soldier too well to insist upon the rectitude of the American case, but he used the lever of his personal friendship with the Mexican president to seek a solution to the diplomatic impasse. To the newspapermen in the capital O'Shaughnessy would say nothing. He was a "dry spring" where news was concerned, he told them. Nor could the reporters find Huerta to interview him, though he did reply to a written request from the *New York Times* to state his side of the case. His cabled answer was concise and unequivocal: "Mexico has controversies with nobody, least of all the great American nation. The Tampico incident has no special importance."[34]

On April 15, by the dint of his persistent efforts, O'Shaughnessy achieved the first break in the dike of Huerta's resistance. At noon he delivered to the Mexican president Wilson's note reciting the three recent and grave "affronts" to American honor and demanding prompt and complete satisfaction. Huerta told O'Shaughnessy that the three incidents were trivial, that they were due to ignorance and certainly not to intention. He could not see, he said, why the president of the United States could not accept his original statement as sufficient. O'Shaughnessy expressed his complete agreement. These were indeed picayunish matters. But he told Huerta quite frankly that he could not afford to stand on "a matter of right," that he must rather "look

[33] *New York Times*, April 20, 1914, 1:4. Arthur S. Link believes that Wilson's intervention was not popularly supported. It is admittedly difficult to test public opinion at any time. Yet it seems clear from letters in the Wilson Papers and from contemporary news accounts that most Americans backed the president.

[34] O'Shaughnessy, *Diplomat's Wife*, 262; *New York Times*, April 16, 1914, 1:6-7.

to the expediency" of coming to a satisfactory arrangement with the United States.

Later that same afternoon, O'Shaughnessy caught Huerta in a more mellow and conciliatory mood. There was another of the many official receptions given by the president at Chapultepec Castle, and many foreign diplomats, including both O'Shaughnessys, were invited. The American chargé d'affaires seized the opportunity to closet himself with Huerta, while, according to Edith O'Shaughnessy, the guests waited for tea for over an hour, with "occasional glances at the closed door." In the anteroom off the main salon Huerta complained vociferously to O'Shaughnessy about the "machinations" of his enemies against him both in the United States and in Mexico. At length, overcome by O'Shaughnessy's persistence, he capitulated. He would agree, he conceded, to a simultaneous salute by batteries of both countries. But he feared to fire first because he believed the United States would not return his salute and thereby humiliate his government. O'Shaughnessy replied that if he were in Huerta's place, he would "get busy and fire the salute" and terminate the crisis. The conference concluded, the guests went into the salon for their tea. Mrs. O'Shaughnessy, stately, almost regal, in her formal gown, walked in on the arm of the president. It was a moment of triumph for the O'Shaughnessys.[35]

Yet O'Shaughnessy's success was more apparent than actual. An agreement for a simultaneous salute was no agreement at all from the American standpoint. What Wilson was demanding was precisely what Huerta was seeking so desperately to avoid—public apology and humiliation. Instead of being pleased with this small gain, Wilson was increasingly vexed with O'Shaughnessy for his friendship with the Mexican president and for the tepidity with

[35] O'Shaughnessy to Bryan, April 15, 1914 /11522; O'Shaughnessy, *Diplomat's Wife*, 267.

which he presented the American case to Huerta. He complained to congressmen at the White House that O'Shaughnessy was often seen riding in Huerta's automobile, not realizing that this was in most instances the only opportunity to see Huerta and to hand him diplomatic dispatches. Wilson would have recalled O'Shaughnessy at once, but he was afraid that the sending of a successor might in some way indicate the recognition of Huerta's government. Though he did not know it, O'Shaughnessy's days of glory were numbered. Wilson waited only for the right moment to relieve him from his post.[36]

The news that Huerta had apparently consented to fire a salute arrived at the State Department in Washington at about 10 a.m. on April 16. Though the dispatch from O'Shaughnessy was perfectly clear—Huerta had agreed to simultaneous salutes—its import was misunderstood by Bryan, who always wanted news to be better than it was. He brought the decoded message to the White House in person. To the reporters gathered in the president's reception room the secretary of state radiated optimism. He "fairly bounced" into the room, announcing happily that he had "good news" for them. He refused to elaborate or to make a statement, though, until he had consulted with the president. After almost an hour, Bryan emerged from Wilson's study wearing a "broad smile." "I believe that I have good news for you," he repeated. "We have just received a dispatch from Mexico City, and the advices are very encouraging." He would say no more at that time.[37]

Upon his return to the State Department, Bryan composed an answer to O'Shaughnessy: "The President is grateful . . . that General Huerta is disposed to bring the incident to a close by complying with Mayo's demand." He gave his assurance that the salute would be returned: "This,

[36] *New York Times,* April 16, 1914, 1:8.
[37] *New York World,* April 17, 1914, 2:1.

I may add, is the invariable custom from which this government would not of course depart." Now that he had agreed to a salute, said Bryan, Huerta should take the matter up at once through the "proper channels."[38]

Huerta's apparent capitulation would have done him no good, however, for too much had happened since Mayo's original demand for the issue to be settled by a simple exchange of salutes. Wilson had mobilized not only the armed forces of the United States (army troops were being assembled in Galveston, Texas, for possible use in Mexico), but public opinion as well, and the stirred-up national emotions could not be turned off like water in a spigot. That afternoon Wilson made it clear in a statement to the press that he was determined that "no similar situation" should arise in the future. The fleet would not be recalled, even though Huerta did accede to the American demands. It would remain in Mexican waters, he said, and every action of Huerta's government which concerned Americans would be examined with a "jaundiced eye." He would no longer permit, Wilson promised, a repetition of the "many manifestations of ill-will and contempt for the United States which Huerta has exhibited in the past." Each time that Huerta "overstepped the bounds of international dignity," he would be "called to account sharply by the United States."[39] In the end, unless Huerta resigned, American forces would be used in Mexico, whether the flag was saluted or not.

Upon the receipt of Bryan's message, O'Shaughnessy realized immediately that Huerta's proposal had been misinterpreted. He conferred at length with the foreign minister, López Portillo y Rojas, who had returned to Mexico City, and in his reply to Bryan, O'Shaughnessy expressed his concern that his previous telegram might have appeared

[38] Bryan to O'Shaughnessy, April 16, 1914 /11522.
[39] *New York World*, April 17, 1914, 1:7-8; 2:1-2.

"ambiguous." Huerta insisted, he said, upon a simultaneous salute of the American and Mexican flags at Tampico, "an absolute coincidence in time in the two actions." He feared that this was the "best arrangement" that could be made. Huerta continued to insist that his position was correct, O'Shaughnessy said, and that the American "marines" had no right to be where they were. And he would not fire a salute of apology, since the Mexicans had done nothing for which to apologize.[40]

This volley of diplomatic dispatches brought deep disappointment to Secretary of State Bryan. Where on the previous day his outlook had been completely sanguine, now he saw little hope for a peaceful solution to the crisis. If Huerta would not fire a salute of apology, Wilson would not hear of a simultaneous exchange of salutes. To agree to this, the president told reporters, would deprive Mexico's action of its significance. He was now abandoning the "generous attitude" which had characterized relations between his administration and Huerta's government for over a year, Wilson said. And as though to underscore the tougher policy initiated by the president, Josephus Daniels announced to the press that the fleet would continue to Mexican waters, its orders unchanged.[41]

Nor did this new and sterner attitude of Wilson move Huerta to further concessions. He had done "everything he was obliged to do," he told O'Shaughnessy. Morelos Zaragoza had made a full apology; there had been an official investigation to determine the extent of Hinojosa's guilt. Huerta said that any nation in the world would have considered these proceedings as "a sufficient satisfaction." But he had gone beyond mere obligations, Huerta insisted, and had offered a simultaneous salute which would signify the "satisfaction with which the two countries see the

40 O'Shaughnessy to Bryan, April 16, 1914 /11532.
41 *New York World*, April 18, 1914, 1:1.

happy end of a conflict which has at no time been really serious." Whatever Bryan might have thought of the proposal for simultaneous salutes, Huerta had not budged from his original position: He would admit no guilt.[42]

To O'Shaughnessy there seemed no course open but military intervention. He told López Portillo y Rojas frankly, almost brutally: "I could see only one reason for the refusal of our demand, in view of the fact that General Huerta had every opportunity to save his face, namely that the cause of the federal government was lost and that foreign intervention was the only fair expectation that could save Mexico from anarchy." And he wrote to Bryan: "I have exerted every influence upon General Huerta, that of my personal friendship, as well as that of my official character. I have canvassed many of his friends and ministers, and I regret most profoundly my failure to bring him to reason."[43]

It was Woodrow Wilson's custom, almost invariable, to play golf each Saturday morning at the Washington Country Club. Despite the critical international situation, Saturday, April 18, was no exception. While he and Dr. Grayson were out on the course, O'Shaughnessy's message of the previous night arrived at the State Department. It was apparent, even to Bryan, that the last slight possibility for a peaceful settlement had vanished. He called the president's secretary, Joseph Tumulty, on the telephone to say that it was imperative that he reach Wilson at once. Tumulty, in turn, called the country club to notify the president that he and Bryan were on their way to meet him. A secret service man carried the message out to Wilson, who was by now at the fourteenth hole. Wilson decided not to wait. Walking "briskly" (according to a newspaper ac-

---

[42] O'Shaughnessy to Bryan, April 17, 1914 /11540.
[43] O'Shaughnessy to Bryan, April 17, 1914 /11540; O'Shaughnessy, *Diplomat's Wife*, 270-273.

count) over the course to the clubhouse, he took his automobile back toward Washington. The two parties met on the Key Bridge near Rosslyn, Virginia, where they stopped so that Bryan and Wilson could discuss this latest development.[44] In a few minutes the president returned to the White House to compose a statement of policy on his own typewriter. It was released to the press at the same time that it was dispatched to O'Shaughnessy.[45]

"General Huerta is still insisting upon doing something less than has been demanded and something less than would constitute an acknowledgment that his representatives were entirely in the wrong in the indignities they have put upon the government of the United States," Wilson wrote. He now presented Huerta with a new ultimatum: If the Mexicans did not yield, agreeing to fire the salute by 6 p.m. of the following day, he would lay the matter before Congress on Monday "with a view of taking such action as may be necessary to enforce the respect due to the nation's flag."

By the time the message reached O'Shaughnessy in Mexico City, it was late afternoon. He had a "free, but strong" translation of the note made in the embassy and then set out to find Huerta. The Mexican president was in none of his "usual haunts," however, and so O'Shaughnessy took the message to López Portillo y Rojas. He begged the foreign minister to make certain that Wilson's ultimatum reached Huerta. López Portillo y Rojas, like O'Shaughnessy, hoped to avoid hostilities between their two countries. In the event that Huerta did agree to the demands set forth in Wilson's letter, he asked, would O'Shaughnessy be willing to sign a protocol guaranteeing that the salute would be returned by the American warships at Tampico? O'Shaughnessy replied that he would. In so doing, he committed a grievous error, for he was consent-

---

[44] *New York Times*, April 19, 1914, 1:8; Baker, *Woodrow Wilson*, 322.
[45] Bryan to O'Shaughnessy, April 18, 1914 /11540.

ing to sign the document without having seen it and, worst of all, without having consulted his superiors.[46]

That evening at 8:20, López Portillo y Rojas entered the door of the American embassy in full diplomatic dress, wearing the bright green and gold sash of his office. He was in an exultant mood. He had finally prevailed upon General Huerta, he said, to accept the terms of the United States. A Mexican battery at Tampico would salute the American flag, upon assurances that the salute would be returned immediately by a warship of the United States flying the pennant of Admiral Mayo. But when the foreign minister handed O'Shaughnessy the proposed protocol, it was at once clear that it was unacceptable to the United States. It enumerated all of the grievances claimed by the American government, but, at the same time, absolved the Mexicans at Tampico of all wrongdoing. Moreover, the protocol was so cleverly worded that, had O'Shaughnessy placed his signature upon it, his action might have been construed as recognition by the United States of Huerta's regime. He would not sign the document, O'Shaughnessy said, until he could consult Washington.[47]

Late Saturday night the president entrained for White Sulphur Springs to bring Mrs. Wilson back to Washington, and he was not in the capital when O'Shaughnessy's message arrived. Secretary of State Bryan was still at the department, however. (He and Mrs. Bryan had given up a planned vacation in Florida until the Mexican crisis was resolved.) The cablegram began to come over the department's wires shortly after 11 p.m., and by the time it had been decoded, it was too late to communicate with Wilson, for the presidential train had already left the Washington station. Bryan cabled O'Shaughnessy at 1 a.m. that the president was out

---

[46] O'Shaughnessy to Bryan, April 18, 1914, State Department Files, National Archives, Post Records, Mexico City, 800/865.

[47] O'Shaughnessy, *Diplomat's Wife*, 276; O'Shaughnessy to Bryan, April 18, 1914 /11555.

of town, and that he could not be reached before morning. He said, however, that Wilson would object "emphatically" to the signing of a protocol or agreement of whatever nature. Mayo's demand, he stressed, "must be accepted unconditionally."[48]

Bryan telephoned Wilson at the Green Briar Hotel early the next morning to report the exchange of messages with O'Shaughnessy. The president gave short shrift to the notion of a settlement by means of a signed protocol. Bryan's reply to O'Shaughnessy, he said, was "exactly what I would have wished it to be. In no case should any concession of any kind in detail or otherwise be made." Wilson asked Bryan to inform Huerta's government that further negotiations were unnecessary.[49]

The Mexicans, too, were disinclined to propose further concessions. When O'Shaughnessy brought Bryan's note to the Foreign Office, López Portillo y Rojas replied that the "Mexican government is not disposed to accede to the unconditional demands of the government of the United States, but is disposed to act according to the terms of the protocol." Although the foreign minister accused him of inconsistency in first consenting and then refusing to sign the protocol, O'Shaughnessy said that as far as he was concerned "the matter was closed."[50]

The diplomatic negotiations between the United States and Mexico had run their course, and there was now no solution to the impasse except military action. The week of note sending and receiving added up to one thing: Neither country had changed its original position in any way.

Over the weekend Wilson remained quietly with his family at White Sulphur Springs, sketching out the address

[48] Baker Chronological File, Box 63, April 19, 1914; *New York World,* April 19, 1914, 1:5-6; *New York Times,* April 20, 1914, 1:6-7; Bryan to O'Shaughnessy, April 19, 1914 /11555.

[49] Wilson to Bryan, April 19, 1914 /11627.

[50] O'Shaughnessy to Bryan, April 19, 1914 /11552; O'Shaughnessy to Bryan, April 19, 1914 /11553.

he would read to a joint session of Congress on Monday. He refused to see reporters or to give any hint of his intentions. Late Sunday night Bryan conferred with the president again by telephone, and Wilson asked him to arrange for an emergency meeting of the cabinet for the next morning. There was little doubt that the president would get what he wanted from Congress—a blank check to deal with Huerta as he saw fit. Before leaving Washington, Wilson had consulted his military advisers on the best way to bring military pressure on Huerta's government short of actual war. The consensus was that the United States should occupy both Tampico and Veracruz and establish a belligerent blockade of the entire east coast. As he made his plans, Wilson expected, in view of the preponderant force of the United States, that the Mexicans would offer no resistance. It was a vain, if pious, hope.[51]

At Tampico, Admiral Mayo and his staff perfected plans for the seizure of the city. His force, which a few days earlier he had not considered sufficient for the task, had been strengthened. The troopship *Hancock* stood off the bar with a contingent of nearly one thousand marines under Colonel J. A. Lejeune. Mayo sent Lejeune ashore with his aide, Major S. D. Butler, to familiarize himself with the terrain surrounding Tampico in anticipation of the landing. He used *Dolphin* and other small vessels in the river to bring inside the bar as many marines as he could. Mayo also took possession of the yacht *Wakiva,* which belonged to the Huasteca Oil Company, to serve as a liaison vessel with the ships anchored outside. The great fleet under Admiral Badger was not expected to arrive at Tampico (Badger's orders still made no mention of Veracruz) before the twenty-first. Even without reinforcements from the Atlantic Fleet, though, Mayo was confident that he now had enough ships and marines at Tampico to carry out

[51] *New York World,* April 20, 1914, 1:5-6.

whatever instructions should come from Washington. On April 20, he received orders from Daniels to clear the Pánuco River of all American merchant vessels. No one doubted that there would soon be military action at Tampico.[52]

The situation at Veracruz was more confused. Fletcher had a much smaller force now than Mayo, and the port was defended by shore installations which, if antiquated, could be used with some effect against the American ships. But also the federal garrison at Veracruz was correspondingly smaller. Though it was a far larger and more important city than Tampico, there was no threat of a rebel attack near Veracruz (the Constitutionalists were still far north of Mexico City), and many troops had been shifted to Tampico to meet the attack there. General Gustavo Maass, the federal commander, had fewer than one thousand men in two regiments. Though Fletcher could reasonably expect to land eventually at Veracruz, there was no indication by April 20 from Washington that a landing was imminent. As it turned out, however, the unexpected happened, and Fletcher was the first to send his men ashore. It was due to a strange twist of fate and had nothing to do with the logic of the situation.

From time to time, William W. Canada had been reporting to the State Department that arms shipments were coming to Huerta's government through the port of Veracruz. On April 18 he cabled Bryan—though the message was not received in Washington until 12:30 a.m. of the nineteenth—that the Ward Line steamer *Mexico* had arrived that day with one thousand cases of ammunition. He mentioned too that another ship, "Ipiranga [*sic*]," would arrive on Tuesday (the twenty-first) with two hundred machine-guns and fifteen million cartridges. During the day follow-

[52] *New York Times,* April 18, 1914, 3:4; *Dolphin* Log, April 17-18, 1914; "Regimental Order No. 1," April 17, 1914, RG 45/659; Mayo, "Memorandum," April 20, 1914, RG 45/659.

ing the receipt of Canada's message, clerks of the State Department tried unsuccessfully to determine the ship's nationality, but, since the name had been misspelled by Canada, it could not be found in either Lloyd's or the Maritime register. It was the fear that Huerta would shortly receive a large quantity of arms, which might enable him to hold out against the rebels indefinitely and which might be used against the Americans, that forced the Wilson government to make a hasty decision. At least for the time being, the plans to take Tampico were abandoned. Instead, all of the power of the United States would be concentrated at Veracruz to stop this one ship.[53]

April 20 was a day of decision for President Wilson. At 8:40 a.m. his train arrived at the Washington station, and, after breakfasting with his family, he spent the morning discussing the Mexican crisis with his aides. He reviewed with his cabinet members the address he would deliver that afternoon to Congress, and indicated to them the quick shift in plans necessitated by the approach of the freighter with ammunition for Huerta. By now the original incident seemed forgotten in the rush to block the arms shipment.[54]

From the White House, Daniels went to the Department of the Navy for several hurried conferences with his naval officers, and at 2 p.m. he radioed orders to Admiral Mayo to proceed with all of the ships under his command (except *Dolphin*) to Veracruz and to be prepared to land upon arrival. *Dolphin* would remain at Tampico as a symbol for the American force there, but would be stationed outside the river so as not to be trapped in the event of trouble. No reason was given Mayo for this radical change in plans. One hour later, similar orders were transmitted to Badger, whose ships had been proceeding toward Tampico at a

[53] Canada to Bryan, April 18, 1914 /11547.
[54] Daniels Diary, April 20, 1914, Daniels Papers; Baker Chronological File, Box 63, April 20, 1914.

leisurely speed of twelve knots in order to accommodate the older and slower vessels. Until now there had been no need for haste. Upon receipt of the new instructions, Badger ordered full steam in all ships and a shift of course toward Veracruz. It was calculated that even at top speed the ships of the Atlantic Fleet could not reach Veracruz before the twenty-second. But Mayo could move his ships from Tampico to Veracruz overnight and could be expected there sometime on the twenty-first, the day the arms shipment would arrive. No one in Washington seemed concerned about the possible effect of the removal of the ships from Tampico or asked Mayo's opinion.[55]

Because of difficulties in radio communication, Mayo did not receive the order from Daniels until late in the evening of the twentieth. The import of this message struck Mayo and his officers with the force of a thunderbolt. It had been a foregone conclusion that they would soon go ashore at Tampico. Their plans were completed; the men alert. The Mexicans in Tampico suspected there would be a landing, and the American colony was certain of it. This sudden new development seemed incomprehensible to Mayo, and he hoped, somehow, that because of the severe static conditions the original order from Washington had been garbled in transmission. So he delayed compliance until he could obtain from Fletcher a confirmation of the text. At the same time, he called Clarence Miller aboard *Dolphin* to inform him that the ships might soon be withdrawn.

Miller found a completely different atmosphere among Mayo's officers. Earlier, as they had labored over their landing plans, they had seemed "joyous" at the prospect of action at Tampico. For many of the men, this would be their initial test under fire. Now they were "downcast and despondent." Admiral Mayo, Miller wrote to Bryan

[55] Daniels to Mayo, April 20, 1914, Miscellaneous Papers, Daniels Papers.

later, "was almost broken hearted." He was "almost in
tears when he informed me of his orders." To Miller, as
well, the situation seemed incredible. Mayo's demands had
created the crisis; there was much anti-American feeling in
Tampico; and there were more than one thousand refugees
in the city who would now be left behind to face alone
and unprotected the wrath of the Mexicans. Miller drew
up a strenuous protest in the name of the American refugees
to be transmitted to the State Department, asking that
Mayo's orders be rescinded. Mayo was more than pleased
to send this message on to Fletcher and, ultimately, to
Washington. But Miller never received an answer to his
protest. The State Department was too busy with the situation at Veracruz. Instead, Wilson reiterated his earlier
warning to Americans in Mexico to leave the country, for
the United States could not guarantee their safety.[56]

Early the next morning Mayo's orders were confirmed,
and he prepared to obey them, however much he might
disagree with the wisdom of withdrawing from Tampico.
To Miller he wrote: "I am helpless." He requested Miller
to hire a pilot in Tampico to take the ships out of the river
at 7:30 a.m. The American consul was extremely reluctant
to cooperate in what seemed to him a most foolish venture.
He procrastinated, so that the naval officers were forced to
find their own pilot. Miller said later: "I would have done
anything possible to have prevented their going out (that
is, anything honorable.)" In Tampico the leaders of the
American colony met to formulate a bitterly worded protest
to the United States government for deserting them and
their valuable properties.[57]

Before all of the American ships in the river had nego-

[56] Miller, "Political Conditions"; Miller to Mayo, April 20, 1914, RG
45/659; Fletcher to Badger, "Report on Occupation of Veracruz," May 13,
1914, Box 255, Daniels Papers (hereafter cited as Fletcher to Badger,
"Report").
[57] Miller, "Political Conditions."

tiated the bar and Admiral Mayo had shifted his flag from *Dolphin* to the battleship *Connecticut,* it was after 10:30 a.m. and much too late to aid Fletcher. Within half an hour Fletcher's marines and bluejackets were going ashore at Veracruz. Assured that Badger would arrive within a day and having confidence that he could deal with the small force of federals at the port, Fletcher, without consulting Washington, told Mayo he might keep most of his ships at Tampico. He did ask for *San Francisco* and *Chester,* however; *San Francisco,* which was too deep to enter the river safely at Tampico, could be used effectively inside the breakwater at Veracruz. Mayo immediately accepted Fletcher's offer, but he was in a quandary as to what action to take. He did not want to leave the Americans in Tampico without protection. Yet he did not dare to take his ships back inside the river for fear this move might be interpreted by the Mexicans in Tampico as the beginning of hostilities. And so he waited, doing nothing, his ships at anchor outside the bar, powerless to aid the refugees in any way.[58]

The mismanagement of Mayo's forces at Tampico was indicative of the lack of any coherent plan in Washington for handling the Mexican situation. Woodrow Wilson seemed content to let each day be sufficient unto itself, so that policy was made, not by the president or the Department of State, but by the events themselves.

President Wilson met with leading members of the two houses at 2 p.m. on April 20 to explain what he wanted from Congress. He read to them the brief message which he would shortly deliver to the joint session. Senator Henry Cabot Lodge, the principal Republican spokesman, commented later: "It seemed to me weak and insufficient, although of course well expressed." Lodge agreed with the president that the time was ripe for intervention in Mexico, but he could not accept the reasons advanced by Wilson.

[58] Fletcher to Badger, "Report."

Where the president confined his animus to Huerta and his "studied contempt" toward the United States, Senator Lodge, in consort with most Republicans, would go into Mexico to protect American lives and property. Wilson said that this might lead to war. Lodge replied that it was war in any event. Wilson stressed the need for immediate action from Congress so that he could intercept the cargo of arms due at Veracruz that evening. When Lodge pointed out that, in stopping the ship, Wilson would be, in effect, allying himself with Villa, the president said that it could not be helped. He refused to listen to Lodge or to accept any change in the proposed resolution. His fight was solely with Huerta, and he did not intend to enter Mexico to protect Americans. The Americans in Mexico, Wilson said, must take their chances or leave.[59]

An hour later the president stood before the two houses of Congress to deliver his message in person. It was an eloquent address, characterized by Wilson's happy choice of the right word at the right time. Yet it added nothing new to that which was already well known, and it demonstrated again how poorly he had kept abreast of affairs in Mexico. Wilson was conveniently vague when discussing what action he would take in Mexico, but he emphasized that it must be against the man Huerta, and not the Mexican people. He reviewed the incident at Tampico which had led to the crisis. But this was not an isolated case, he said. "A series of incidents have recently occurred, which cannot but create the impression that the representatives of General Huerta were willing to go out of their way to show disregard for the dignity and rights of this government and felt perfectly safe in doing what they pleased, making free to show in many ways their irritation and contempt." The president referred to the mail orderly at

[59] Henry Cabot Lodge, *The Senate and the League of Nations* (New York, 1925), 13-14.

Veracruz who was "thrown into jail," and the censor who had withheld an official dispatch until it was "peremptorily" demanded by the American chargé d'affaires. "So far as I can learn, such wrongs and annoyances have been suffered to occur only against representatives of the United States." And it seemed that the "government of the United States was being singled out and might be singled out with impunity for slights and affronts in retaliation for its refusal to recognize General Huerta . . . as provisional president of the Republic of Mexico."

Wilson emphasized the danger that these "offenses" would grow worse until "something happened of so gross and intolerable a sort as to lead directly and inevitably to armed conflict." It was necessary, he said, to impress upon Huerta "that no further occasion for explanation and professed regrets should arise." He demanded from Huerta, not only a salute of apology, but a "new spirit," so that such incidents did not occur in the future. It was true, he said, that he did not need the consent of Congress "to enforce respect for our government." But he did wish to act in "close conference and cooperation with both the Senate and the House." He asked the approval of Congress, therefore, to use the armed forces of the United States in such ways and to such an extent as might be necessary "to obtain from General Huerta and his adherents the fullest recognition of the rights and dignity of the United States." Wilson ignored the question of protecting American interests and lives in Mexico, and he did not reveal the imminent approach of the cargo of arms. Instead, he stressed throughout his address that American honor must be restored through armed action against General Huerta. When he had concluded his address, the president retired from the chamber to a standing ovation from the members of the two houses.[60]

[60] *Foreign Relations Papers, 1914* (Washington, 1922), 474-476.

There was virtually no opposition to the resolution in the House of Representatives, and it was passed with little ado in the form Wilson had asked. In the Senate, however, it was another matter. A group of Republicans, led by Elihu Root and Lodge, had prepared a substitute measure, which approved the use of force in Mexico, but for a much stronger reason, to protect American lives and property. The Republicans would intervene, not alone against Huerta, but in the areas controlled by the revolutionaries as well. The substitute measure had no chance of passage, for the Senate was firmly in control of the Democrats, but there was sufficient Republican strength to delay action on the president's resolution. The senators debated until well past midnight of the twentieth with no decision reached on either measure. As it turned out, Wilson could not wait for the senators. Events in Mexico forced his hand, and he was led to intervene without the formal approval of the contentious upper chamber. The approval came later (by a straight party vote), as the president had known that it would, but by then the resolution only consented to a *fait accompli*. American troops were already on Mexican soil.

While the senators wrangled into the night, Wilson conferred with Bryan, Daniels, Secretary of War Lindley M. Garrison, and the army and navy chiefs of staff to complete plans for the occupation of Veracruz. At the conclusion of their meeting, the president retired for the night, without waiting for a decision in the Senate. Daniels went to his office in the Department of the Navy, where he worked until after midnight. Sometime after 2 a.m. on the twenty-first a coded message from Consul Canada began clicking over the wire into the State Department. He now correctly identified the approaching ship as the German liner *Ypir-anga*. It would be landing early that morning, he said, and there were three trains waiting at the dock to speed the arms to Mexico City. This report galvanized the department to quick action. The news was telephoned to Bryan at his home, who in turn called the White House. The servants there were at first disinclined to wake the president, but Bryan finally prevailed upon them to do so. Though roused from his sleep, Wilson did not hesitate. He told Daniels, who by now was also on the wire, to order Fletcher to seize the customhouse at Veracruz immediately. In that way the ammunition could be prevented from falling into Huerta's hands.[61]

And so the line which separates diplomacy from hostilities was crossed in the dark hours of a spring morning with the utterance of a single sentence by the president of the United States. It was not a difficult decision to make. There had been ample preparation for it. Wilson knew, when he went to bed the previous night, that it was only a matter of hours before a landing would be made. There were no phantasms of doubt or uncertainty to disturb the president, for he knew that the Mexicans would not resist. There would be no firing, no bloodshed. Only Huerta would be harmed, and for this, Mexico would thank the United States. As Wilson's friend and confidant, Colonel Edward House, had told him a few days before: "If a man's house was on fire he should be glad to have his neighbors come in and help him put it out, provided they did not take his property, and it should be the same with nations. If Mexico understood that our motives were unselfish, she should not object to our helping adjust her unruly household." These were Woodrow Wilson's sentiments, too.[62]

[61] Baker, *Woodrow Wilson*, IV, 328-329; Canada to Bryan, April 20, 1914 /11564; *New York Times*, April 22, 1914, 1:1-4; Daniels to Fletcher, April 21, 1914, Miscellaneous Papers, Daniels Papers.
[62] House Diary, April 15, 1914.

THREE

Bloodshed at Veracruz

IF WOODROW WILSON had little understanding of Mexico or the Mexican people, he knew next to nothing about the city of Veracruz, whose seizure he now ordered. He asked no questions, made no plans, sought no advice. Its character did not concern him. It did concern intimately, however, the several hundred officers and men under the command of Admiral Frank F. Fletcher who would presently be called upon to occupy the port.

Veracruz was a city of contrasts, of old and new, sordid and sublime, commerce and concupiscence. At first glance, either from the sea or from a train carriage descending from the central plateau, the city was an artist's delight. In fair weather the sky and sea seemed to vie for ascendancy, each matching or surpassing the other, azure blue for emerald green, filmy cloud for whitecap and spume. At the entrance to the harbor the ancient fortress of San Juan de Ulua, embraced on either side by the great arms of the seawalls, mounted guard over the city, its massive, white-washed walls starkly reflecting the glaring sunlight. The entire waterfront was of concrete, faced with a coping of gray Scandinavian granite blocks. Inside the harbor, jaunty gray and white gulls and lugubrious gray pelicans rode the slight waves or dropped in screaming dives upon a hapless fish or a floating morsel of food. Far above the city and the harbor were the *zopilotes,* innocuous and almost beautiful at such a distance, soaring majestically in great circles, rising with the thermal currents ever higher, as though, defying gravity, they must leave the earth itself.[1]

Behind the harbor works the city nestled in low, sandy hills which were lush and green throughout the year. The buildings of Veracruz took their colors from nature—various shades of bright blue, green, or red, as well as muted pastels. That they were gaudy was not to be gainsaid, though—in the tropics—they were nonetheless tasteful. Close by the waterfront were the commercial and governmental buildings, the hotels, the markets, and the churches. Almost all were squat, two or three stories in height at most. Only the churches and the great lighthouse were taller. Behind were the residences of the wealthier classes, the newer homes built of brick, granite, or concrete, the more venerable of white coral from the reefs outside the harbor. Some wore quaint wooden balconies, painted green or pink, and most had thick doors of carved wood and studded metal, shut firmly against the outside world. All the lower windows were barred because of the ubiquitous Mexican sneak-thieves. From the patios in the centers of these houses grew tall coconut palms—the same graceful trees which grew in such profusion in the parks and plazas of the city and along the Paseo de los Cocos. The streets were romantically narrow—many had been laid out in the time of the vice-roys—and, except for the asphalted areas closest to the waterfront, were constructed of cobblestones. On the fringes of Veracruz were the huts of the poor, of native wood or of thatch. The city was already beginning to encroach

[1] *Terry's Guide to Mexico* (Boston, 1909), 473-474.

into the sandhills. And beyond these hills, fifty miles in the interior, loomed the perpetual snow of the Pico de Orizaba, at 18,300 feet Mexico's loftiest mountain. Could the visitor see all of this, and solely this, he would depart convinced that Veracruz was an earthly paradise, that it possessed a beauty beyond all imagination.[2]

Veracruz was indeed beautiful, but it was dirty and unkempt as well. On closer inspection the fortress of San Juan de Ulua was no longer dazzling white. The whitewash on the walls had flaked off under the impact of storm winds and salt water, and they were now drably gray. The military forces on the island had once protected the city—or had sought to protect it—against foreign invaders, but they now mounted guard over hapless convicts. The fort had been turned into a vile, filthy, and seemingly uninhabitable federal prison. A few of the inmates had been convicted of criminal charges, but most had been sent to San Juan de Ulua by Huerta's government when they tried to avoid service in the army. Under primitive and unsanitary conditions they lived in dank, cavernous holes, many scores of men crowded into a single cell. There was neither light nor air, except from one aperture left in the solid stone ceiling. The stones of the cells (in some places the walls were ten feet thick) were encrusted with salt, and evidently the walls and floors had not been cleaned for centuries. The occasional visitor to San Juan de Ulua—Edith O'Shaughnessy was one of these in 1914—was invariably nauseated by the fetid odors emanating from the bowels of the prison. And his heart must have sickened at the sight of dirty, emaciated hands clawing up, or at the muffled sounds of voices thirty feet below pleading for cigarettes, food, or simply for mercy. But there was no mercy, no

2 *Terry's Guide,* 474; Richard Harding Davis, "When Is a War Not a War?" *Scribner's Magazine,* LVI (July, 1914), 44; War Portfolio No. 1, Information Section (Mexico), GBR; "Veracruz: A Crusade for Decency," *Outlook,* CVII (July 4, 1914), 527-528.

surcease from suffering, and seemingly no hope in San Juan de Ulua. The prison cast a malevolent shadow across the harbor and the city.[3]

As the visitor debarked from his ship or left the railway station at the waterfront, it was equally apparent that the harbor works, though modern, were neglected also. Refuse from the city and the ships, as well as storm-tossed debris, floated in pockets between the wharves, bits of garbage, coconut hulls, fronds of trees, papers. The waterfront was alive with vultures, hundreds of them, crowding the stone coping of the seawall, their dark wing and tail feathers trimmed to the wind, pushing ill-naturedly for more favorable positions on the stone steps to snatch up some edible morsel from the water. Now seen up close, the ugliness of the *zopilotes* seemed an affront to mankind. Naked black heads with villainous eyes, scaly necks like coiled snakes protruded from the hunched shoulders. On land the vultures' awkwardness belied the grace of their companions soaring above the city. Wings akimbo they hopped clumsily on skinny, crooked legs, and they reeked perpetually of carrion. Despite their repulsiveness, the *zopilotes* were tolerated by the people of Veracruz because they were nature's scavengers, cleaning up piles of garbage cast heedlessly into the streets, or dead animals left where they had died. There was a fine of five pesos, levied by the city fathers, for anyone who dared harm a *zopilote*.[4]

This intimate relationship of man to vulture, the rational creature's resigned acceptance of the proximity of evil, characterized the Veracruzano's general outlook. Among the populace of the city, and in the government as well, there was a pronounced *laissez faire* attitude toward the problems of daily life. No one seemed to concern himself,

[3] O'Shaughnessy, *Diplomat's Wife*, 232-234; *Mexican Herald*, May 2, 1914, 4:4; May 28, 1914, 4:4-5; Arthur Ruhl, "The Unfinished Drama," *Collier's Magazine*, LIII (May 30, 1914), 8.
[4] *Terry's Guide*, 472.

for example, with matters of sanitation or public health. Flies covered the meats, fish, and other foods carelessly exposed for sale in the market. It was not surprising that fly-borne diseases, such as dysentery, were endemic in Veracruz. Animals came and went as they pleased, even in the best restaurants. One visitor in 1914, a member of the American Red Cross, found chickens roosting over the cooking stoves in the kitchen of a prominent hotel. On the menu for the day the management proclaimed (on the English half of the food list) its specialty: "Chicken cooked in its own moist." Pariah dogs, singly or in packs, skulked through the streets, searching for garbage, fighting over the carcass of a mule or another dog, their protruding ribcases giving grim evidence of their perpetual hunger. The vultures made themselves rudely at home throughout the city, following the dogs to the refuse piles outside the restaurants and even into the center of the market, perching on the window ledges of the hotels and the cupolas and crosses of the parochial church, and invading private residences. While he was in Veracruz, the visitor would never be more than a few feet from these foul-smelling birds.[5]

Veracruz was a thriving city and, in many respects, a progressive city as well. It was Mexico's principal port. Except for the oil of Tampico and the ores of the north country, almost all of the imports and exports passed through its docks and warehouses. To hold Veracruz was to possess the largest part of the revenues available to the national government. Yet if trade flourished, so did vice, tended with loving care by the city's officials. About half of the business establishments of Veracruz were cantinas, retailing pulque or other more intoxicating beverages: rum, tequila, mezcal, and imported whiskies. And prostitution,

[5] *Terry's Guide*, 473; Charles Jenkinson, "Vera Cruz, What American Occupation Has Meant to a Mexican Community," *Survey*, XXXIII (November 7, 1914), 133-138.

as it must be in any port, was a lucrative and thriving industry, controlled and protected by the city's government. There were also the lesser vices—if indeed they may be called such in Mexico—cockfighting, gambling, and the bullring. For those whose pursuit of pleasure was less lascivious or rigorous, Veracruz was a winter resort, especially attractive to Mexicans who hoped to escape for a few days the more strenuous life in the higher altitudes. It was justly famous for its hotels, its seafood, and its beaches. If one could ignore or overlook the filth—and most Mexicans did—life could be pleasant in Veracruz. Pleasant, that is, except in the summer. Then the dank heat, with temperatures at times over 100 degrees, the flies and mosquitoes, and the malarial attacks drove out to sea or back to the mountains those who were not forced to reside there.

Founded by Hernán Cortés in 1519, Veracruz was the oldest city in Mexico. It was also, throughout its long history, a most attractive victim of invaders from without. Despite the formidable walls of San Juan de Ulua, the city was violated often in the four centuries of its existence. Though Veracruz was voted "four times honorable" by the national congress for its resistance against foreign aggression, the legislators' vote was an ironic recognition of the fact that the city had been singularly unsuccessful in repelling invaders. During the colonial era, Veracruz was repeatedly sacked by pirates, French, English, and even Spanish. John Hawkins and Sir Francis Drake plundered the city in 1568 for the glory of Queen Elizabeth. In 1683 the port was captured and pillaged by the notorious French pirate, Laurent de Gaff—known to the Spanish as Lorencillo. He locked up some 1,500 Veracruzanos in the parochial church while he robbed their homes and businesses, and many died of suffocation before the doors of the church were reopened. Later in the century the Spaniard Nicolás de Agramonte left 300 people from the city to die outside the harbor on the Isle of Sacrifices. In the 1820's when Mexico was winning its independence from Spain, loyal troops at San Juan de Ulua turned the guns of the fort on the helpless city. The forces of Louis Philippe occupied Veracruz in 1838 in a dispute over French claims against the Mexican government, and the American army of General Winfield Scott passed through the port in 1847 on its way to Mexico City. Seemingly neither the guns of the fortress nor the people of Veracruz were a deterrent to a successful invasion.[6]

Nor did nature's furies spare Veracruz. Many times in a year the coast was buffeted by the winds and rains of a norther. These storms might last for two or more days, and while the gales raged, it was dangerous to be abroad. Everything not lashed down had to be put to the lee of large buildings. The coconut palms of the plazas and principal avenues, their ragged fronds testimony to previous storms, strained at their roots, and many were toppled or were hurled into the sea. In 1856 a norther destroyed most of the ships at anchor inside the harbor. Despite the breakwaters, the winds and the mountainous waves drove the vessels against the reefs and rocks to the south, dashing them to bits, and several hundred sailors lost their lives in the storm. The construction of the new harbor by the government of Porfirio Díaz gave protection now from the waves. But during the most violent moments of a norther there was still danger from winds whose velocity might exceed 100 miles an hour. Ships tied up at the wharves had need to look to their ground tackle. While the winds blew, it was safer to ride out the storm at anchor outside the harbor. As for light vessels, it was impossible to move these until the storm had subsided. The most violent storms came between November and March, but a norther might

[6] *Terry's Guide*, 479; Manuel B. Trens, *Historia de la H. Ciudad de Veracruz* (Mexico City, 1955), *passim*.

be expected at almost any time of the year, except mid-summer.[7]

This, then, with all its violent contrasts, was Veracruz in 1914. The venture, which must have seemed so simple to Wilson in the early morning hours of April 21, proved more complex and far more difficult than he dreamed possible.

The morning of April 21, 1914, broke gray and ominous at Veracruz. There was no hint of sun, and dark clouds billowed and tumbled across the sky, driven by strong winds from the north. Inside the harbor the gray waters uneasily reflected the sullen skies, while outside the concrete breakwaters the sea was choppy, as whitecaps were turned up by the gusty winds. The battleships *Utah* and *Florida* rode uneasily at anchor, heaving and grumbling against their tackle in the great swells. Scores of sharks could be seen, their dorsal fins cleaving the whitecaps. Surely, thought Fletcher, a storm was imminent, possibly a norther. In that event it would be impossible to launch small boats from the vessels outside the breakwaters. If he was to make a landing at Veracruz, since both *Utah* and *Florida* were too large to pass inside the harbor, it must come before the storm hit the port.[8]

Throughout the night the men and officers of the Fourth Division were alert, awaiting orders from Washington. At 8:00 a.m. the radio operator of *Florida* brought Fletcher the laconic message of Josephus Daniels: "Seize custom house. Do not permit war supplies to be delivered to Huerta government or any other party." The decision to land troops at Veracruz instead of Tampico had caught Fletcher shorthanded. Badger's fleet was still a day's sailing to the north, and most of the ships permanently stationed in Mex-

[7] *Terry's Guide,* 472, 477; War Portfolio No. 1, Information Section (Mexico), GBR.
[8] *Florida* Log, April 21, 1914.

ican waters were now with Mayo at Tampico. Fletcher could wait for *Ypiranga*—scheduled to arrive at 10:30 that morning—and for the reinforcements from Badger and Mayo before effecting a landing with a greatly augmented force. This was his preference. But the glowering weather forced his hand, and he made the decision to land immediately.[9]

Admiral Fletcher had at his disposal the marine contingents from *Prairie* (a gunboat) and *Utah* and *Florida*, and the battalion of seamen from *Florida*. In all, there were 787 officers and men, 502 of these marines, in the landing party formed under the command of William R. Rush, *Florida's* captain. Fletcher directed *Utah* to remain outside the harbor with its battalion of blue jackets aboard, to waylay *Ypiranga* and, if necessary, to follow it to another port to prevent the delivery of the arms to Huerta. At 9:00 a.m., as the men made their preparations for disembarking, Commander H. O. Stickney, *Prairie's* captain, went ashore to apprise the American consul, William W. Canada, of the impending military action.[10]

Canada, a veteran of many years' service with the State Department, had already foreseen the news from Fletcher. He had been in close contact with his superiors in Washington during the night and was ready for any eventuality. On the previous day he had published to the members of the American colony in Veracruz a warning of possible hostilities. Canada chartered the passenger ships *Mexico* and *Esperanza* in the name of the United States government and advised all Americans to go aboard to be in a place of safety. Many had done so, but most preferred to remain in the city, not anticipating difficulties. Shortly before 9:30 a.m., Stickney entered the consulate. The landing would commence at approximately 11:00 a.m., he told Canada, but only the harbor facilities, that is, the docks,

[9] Daniels to Fletcher, April 21, 1914, Miscellaneous Papers, Daniels Papers; Fletcher to Badger, "Report."

[10] Fletcher to Badger, "Report"; *Prairie* Log, April 21, 1914.

the railroad station, and the customhouse, would be occupied. In order to avoid any possibility of trouble with the Mexicans, the Americans would not proceed into the city. He asked Canada, when he could see the landing party of *Prairie* shoving off, to notify the federal commander in Veracruz, General Gustavo Maass, that the Americans were occupying the port.[11]

At the same time a party from *Prairie* was put ashore at San Juan de Ulua to warn the commander of the federal prison (there was an armed guard of 160 men on the island) against any hostile move to thwart the American landing. He was told that the large guns of the battleships lying at close range could be turned on the fort. The American officer emphatically cautioned him against using any torpedoes. The Mexican commander, recognizing the superior strength of the American forces, said he understood the situation. He replied with dignity that if he were fired upon, he would be forced to return the American fire.[12]

As Stickney returned to his ship, Canada took up his station on the roof of the American consulate to watch with fieldglasses for the moment when the boats of the fleet would cast off. The consulate building, which was on the corner of Morelos and Montesinos and across from the principal railroad station, faced the waterfront, and the rooftop offered Canada a superb view of the entire city, as well as the harbor. Before him lay the great sun-seared plaza, edged by a few palm trees, dejected and weatherbeaten. Laborers on the large pier number four, directly in front of the consulate, prepared for the departure of the Ward liner *Mexico,* for the vessel had been ordered by the port officials to clear its berth for the approaching *Ypiranga.* At 10:15, Canada could see *Mexico,* with many Mexican

[11] William W. Canada, "Report on the Occupation of Veracruz by the American Forces," August 11, 1914 /12977 (hereafter cited as Canada, "Report").
[12] *Prairie* Log, April 21, 1914.

and American refugees aboard, move outside the break-water and drop its anchor near the two battleships. *Esperanza*, also carrying a few Americans, remained at its mooring at the Sanitary wharf. In the railroad station and on the dock, three trains, their engines steamed up, awaited *Ypiranga's* cargo of arms. In the city itself, life seemed normal.[13]

To the south—Canada's right—could be seen the main hotels, carrying on business as usual; the great tower of the lighthouse, almost at the water's edge; the market area; and the old parochial church. Behind these was a park, the Benito Juárez plaza, with a statue of the former president, and, adjacent to the park, a school for naval cadets. In the foreground, between the larger plaza and the lighthouse, were the customhouse sheds. Here, too, preparations were being made for receiving the arms shipment to Mexico City.

In the market there was no anticipation of trouble. Housewives and servants haggled with the shopkeepers and vendors over the price of a chicken, a red snapper, a few chiles, a tiny mound of limes, oranges, shaddocks, or avocados. The city government under Porfirio Díaz had begun the construction of a new, modern market, but, with the advent of the revolution, it had never been finished. Naked children played among the half-completed stalls or in the adjacent streets. Despite the threatening weather, it was already beginning to get hot in Veracruz.

A few blocks away, under the *portales*, the covered walk in front of the city's principal hotels, life was gayer, more carefree. Mexicans and Americans sat at the sidewalk tables, ordering a late breakfast or enjoying an early drink. Large electric ceiling fans in the arcades whirled welcome breezes and dispersed the flies. Through the streets newsboys hawked their morning newspapers (there was no public hint of the impending difficulty), and shoeshine boys, dirty

[13] Canada to Bryan, April 21, 1914 /11591.

and unkempt, added their cries to the din and clatter. Beggars, some blind, some infirm, some simply indigent, their palms outstretched, whined for a few *centavitos* from the more fortunate passersby. Donkeys jogged leisurely from door to door, bearing in their leather panniers large tin jugs of fresh, and probably contaminated, milk. Most of the shops were open, and the servant girls, their black braided hair half hidden under their *rebozos*, hastened to make their purchases before the rain. In the schools the children chanted their lessons in shrill unison. In short, it was a day like any other day to the populace of Veracruz —hot, noisy, colorful, and dirty.[14]

At 11:12 a.m., Canada saw through his glasses the first boatload of marines from *Prairie* lowered into the water of the inner harbor. Soon the entire harbor was alive, as motor launches lumbered ashore towing long strings of boats, all loaded with marines and bluejackets from *Utah* and *Florida*. Canada hurried to the telephone below to put through his call to General Maass. For whatever reason, since his government had advised him to be prepared for any emergency, Maass seemed surprised. "No! It cannot be!" he cried. Canada assured Maass that the American troops would go no farther than the waterfront area, and that they would not fire at the Mexicans unless they themselves were fired upon. He requested Maass to remain in the city and to "cooperate with the naval forces in maintaining order." The American consul stressed that Fletcher's strength was "overwhelming," warning Maass that the Mexicans should not attempt to resist the occupation. The federal commander replied that his orders from Mexico City did not permit him to surrender. He asked Canada for a conference, but Canada said that this was impossible, since the landing had already started. General Maass then began to prepare for a token resistance against the Americans. De-

[14] *Terry's Guide*, 474-475; Ruhl, "Unfinished Drama," 22.

spite the hopes of Woodrow Wilson and the warning of Fletcher, the occupation would not be unopposed.[15]

When he had concluded his conversation with General Maass, Canada called the collector of the port to ask his cooperation in the seizure of *Ypiranga's* cargo. Although the Mexican official promised Canada that he would stay to take charge of the customs warehouses after the American landing, he did not fulfill his promise. The mayor of Veracruz and the chief of police also assured Canada that they would remain to help the Americans maintain order in the city. But after the landing they could not be found. What Fletcher and Canada did not know was that a Mexican law—from the days of the French occupation and of Maximilian—provided severe punishment for any Mexican public official who served an invader. The Americans could expect little spirit of cooperation among the officials of Veracruz.[16]

Although General Maass subsequently reported to his superiors in the Ministry of War that he had exhorted his men and the people of Veracruz to action against the Americans, it is evident that he had no intention of putting up more than a token resistance to the invasion. He had fewer than one thousand troops under his command, and these were of poor quality. For several days, because of persistent rumors of possible American intervention, he had been filling his lines with prisoners taken from San Juan de Ulua to replace the men shifted to Tampico. These new recruits were completely untrained and untrustworthy, for they had been sentenced to prison in the first place precisely because they had not wanted to serve in Huerta's army. There were two regular army units stationed in Veracruz, which at full strength might have made the American landing difficult. They were the Eighteenth Regiment of

15 Canada, "Report"; *New York World,* May 3, 1914, 3:1-2.
16 Canada, "Report."

General Luis B. Becerril and the Nineteenth Regiment, commanded by General Francisco A. Figueroa. The military barracks were located on the Plaza Zamora, between Independencia and Cinco de Mayo, about one mile from the pier where the main American force would land. Adjacent was the military prison, "La Galera."[17]

As General Maass entered the barracks of the Nineteenth Regiment, the first officer he chanced to see was Lieutenant Colonel Albino Rodríguez Cerrillo. He ordered Rodríguez Cerrillo to take some of the men of his regiment along Calle Independencia—where their movement would be screened from the American forces—to the terminal mole (pier number four) "to repel the invasion." At the same time, he directed General Figueroa to deploy the rest of his troops around the barracks and the headquarters building, holding them in readiness for action. In the barracks of the Eighteenth Regiment he charged General Becerril to distribute arms—Maass had a good supply of Mausers and Winchester rifles—to the people of Veracruz, while Lieutenant Colonel Manuel Contreras was to furnish weapons to the prisoners in "La Galera." When he gave the order, said Maass, the prisoners and the citizens would march along Cinco de Mayo, paralleling the movement of Rodríguez Cerrillo's men, to the dock area. Maass did not think it necessary to provide his men with a battle plan. Instead, the method of resistance was left up to the individual officers. Meanwhile, Maass sent a courier to Los Cocos radio station, outside the city, with a dispatch for the minister of war, General Aurelio Blanquet, informing him of the American invasion and asking for further instructions.[18]

[17] Gustavo Maass to Secretaría de Guerra y Marina, April 22, 1914, Archivo de Defensa Nacional, Expediente Número XI/481.5/315, Caja 148 (all of the following dispatches of General Maass bear the same file number); *New York World*, May 3, 1914, 3:1-2.
[18] Maass to Secretaría de Guerra y Marina, April 22, 1914; *New York World*, May 3, 1914, 3:1-2; Maass to Secretaría de Guerra y Marina, May 17, 1914.

In view of the superior strength of the American navy, Blanquet directed Maass to pull back his small force and not to resist. He was to take his men, said Blanquet, to Tejería, a small town on the rail line to Mexico City about ten miles from Veracruz, and await developments there. But it was already too late for words of caution from Mexico City. Foolhardiness, valor, and national pride had won the day at Veracruz. By the time Maass had received Blanquet's reply, the men of Contreras and Rodríguez Cerrillo had obeyed their commander's first order. They had tried, however ineffectually, to halt the landing operations. Despite Blanquet's instructions, then, and despite Maass' withdrawal, there was really no hope that Veracruz could be spared a bloodletting. When the Mexicans fired, the Americans retaliated. And once hostilities began, even of a limited nature, there was no possibility that the occupation could be confined to the waterfront areas. The entire city and its population became involved in the fighting between the two forces. In this, President Wilson had seriously miscalculated.[19]

Completely oblivious of Maass' intentions, Captain Rush shepherded his boatloads of fighting men toward the Ward Line's great pier number four. At precisely 11:20 the first boat from *Prairie* scraped the landing platform, and eager marines and sailors, their rifles in readiness, scrambled up the granite steps on the double. Within minutes the other boats tied up at the Ward pier or at one of the smaller Fiscal wharfs to the south to discharge their contingents. Attracted by the long strings of boats converging into the harbor, hundreds of Mexicans and Americans gathered at the edge of the seawall to watch the landing operations. The Mexicans were curious, though they showed no hostility. The Americans, most of whom had been fervently

[19] Maass to Secretaría de Guerra y Marina, May 17, 1914; *New York World,* May 3, 1914, 3:1-2.

hoping for intervention, seemed in a gala mood. They cheered the arrival of each boat, while one woman waved a small American flag enthusiastically. The venture had begun auspiciously, as the marine and bluejacket parties, led by Marine Colonel W. C. Neville, fanned out from the dock area across the brown grassy plaza toward their objectives. Not a shot was fired.[20]

As soon as the Mexicans began to realize the import of the landing, however, the atmosphere of festivity began to change. The crowds at the waterfront fell back along the adjacent streets and under the Portales to continue watching in silence. Shopkeepers rang down the iron doors that covered and protected their windows. School children were sent home by their teachers. In the market the vendors carefully folded their cloth awnings and gathered up their heaps of fruits or vegetables. Even the vultures seemed to sense the impending trouble. They retired from the streets as though for the night to roosts on building ledges or in trees and rudely crowded the arms of the white cross and the tiled cupolas of the parochial church. From their points of vantage they kept close watch on the proceedings below. The city grew quiet and expectant.

The first task of the American forces was to seize the railroad terminal, which lay to the immediate north of the docks. Fletcher hoped to get control of the trains before Maass could withdraw them. He was too late. Major Diego E. Zayas, the military chief at the station, had already taken the fired-up engines and most of the rolling stock to Tejería. Neville's men found only two old, disabled locomotives and a few coaches and sleeping cars, which Zayas had abandoned in his haste to leave before the arrival of the Americans. Captain Rush then occupied the Terminal Hotel alongside the station to use as his headquarters. Soon navy

[20] Canada, "Report"; *Washington Post*, April 22, 1914, 1:5-6; *New York Herald*, April 22, 1914, 1:7-8; Fletcher to Badger, "Report."

signalmen, from the flat rooftop of the hotel, were wig-wagging messages to the ships in the harbor, and communications were established between the land forces and Admiral Fletcher on *Florida*. As the rail terminal was taken without incident, other marines and bluejackets loped across the plaza toward the post office building and the customhouse sheds and down the streets paralleling the railroad tracks to the city's power station. One squad of marines was detailed to take charge of the cable station on Montesinos behind the American consulate.[21]

Inside the cable station there was a frantic scramble by civilians and newspapermen trying to get messages to the United States through the censor. The Mexican official refused to pass any cablegrams, even for members of the press. At 11:45 an armed marine corporal, followed by his men, entered to announce: "I take possession of this office and cable in the name of the United States government." The censor arose from his desk, bowed profoundly to the corporal, and said, shrugging his shoulders: "It is useless to resist, señor. I obey." It had taken but a few minutes to occupy the railroad and cable stations, and there was still no sign of trouble for the American forces.[22]

As the largest contingent of marines and sailors moved along Morelos toward their main objective, the customhouse, the only sounds to be heard in the streets were the dull, rhythmic tread of their boots and the barked orders of their officers. Along Independencia and under the Portales at the Hotel Diligencia, Mexican soldiers quietly trained their rifles on the advancing Americans. At the corner of Independencia and Emparán a group of Contreras' men lay on the rough cobbles, scorning to take cover

[21] Canada, "Report"; Fletcher to Badger, "Report"; Maass to Secretaría de Guerra y Marina, May 17, 1914; Justino M. Palomares, *La invasión yanqui en 1914* (Mexico City, 1940), 33-35.
[22] *Washington Post*, April 22, 1914, 1:5-6.

or to erect a barricade. Liberated prisoners and some venturesome civilians had scaled the rooftops of hotels and office buildings intent on sniping at the invaders. These few Mexicans, scarcely more than a hundred in all, were loyally obeying their commander's decision. At 11:57 the head of the American column reached Emparán and moved into the line of fire of Contreras' men. At that moment an unknown Mexican soldier carefully squeezed his trigger, and the first shot cleaved the silence. In that instant, all hope for a peaceful occupation of Veracruz perished. The shot was followed by a fusillade of fire from various quarters of the city. A navy signalman, flagging a message from the roof of the Terminal Hotel to the ships, fell mortally wounded. He was the first casualty of the invasion.[23]

For most of the sailors and many of the marines, this was their first taste of combat. Though they had been taking normal, textbook precautions in that they moved swiftly from point to point, they were nonetheless careless. They were bunched together, presenting fine targets for the enemy riflemen. Had the Mexicans been better marksmen or had they used their machineguns, the American casualties would have been heavy. As it was, only four Americans were killed and twenty more wounded on the first day of the invasion. Yet, despite the certain knowledge that they now faced armed resistance, the Americans, particularly the seamen, fought crudely and ineptly—if with valor— into the second day. The crew from *Florida* and *Utah* could not accustom themselves to the tactics of street fighting, nor could they resist the continued temptation to move against the enemy as though in close-order drill. On at least one occasion the sailors mistakenly fired at their own comrades, moving in another quarter of the city. As for the

[23] *El País,* April 26, 1914, 2:1; *El Imparcial,* April 26, 1914, 1:5-7, and April 27, 1914, 5:4-5; *La Opinión* (Veracruz), April 22, 1914, 1:3; Maass to Secretaría de Guerra y Marina, May 17, 1914.

Mexicans, they put up only haphazard opposition, and most of the regular troops followed Maass to Tejería by nightfall, leaving the defense of the city to the civilians and the armed prisoners.[24]

With the first fusillade of shots the Americans took cover to return the fire of the enemy—both real and imaginary. They fired at windows, at rooftops, into church steeples, and along the streets and the colonnades of hotels, wherever they suspected the presence of a Mexican rifleman. It is not surprising that there were far more casualties among the bystanders than among the combatants. The Mexican resistance was particularly difficult to cope with, since some of the fire came from snipers concealed in the hotels and in the buildings lining Morelos and the other principal streets of the city. To protect themselves, a group of marines battered down the iron barricade of a Spanish import house, the Barquín company, and dragged out sacks of rice and coffee to form barricades in the streets. (At the same time, large quantities of chocolate, cigars, cigarettes, and other goods disappeared from the warehouse.) Machineguns were set up at the main intersections, and a light fieldpiece was placed in front of the American consulate. When Mexicans were observed firing from the Benito Juárez monument before the naval school, a few well-aimed cannon shots drove them away. The American fire also broke off one of the eagles decorating the statue and marred the inscription attributed to Mexico's great Liberal: "Respect for the rights of others is peace."[25]

With continued enemy opposition, it was apparent to Fletcher that he could no longer afford to hold back *Utah's* battalion. At 12:45 p.m. he directed the sailors of the battleship to begin landing operations at once to reinforce

[24] Canada, "Report"; Fletcher to Badger, "Report"; Lowell Thomas, *Old Gimlet Eye* (New York, 1933), 179.
[25] *El Imparcial,* April 26, 1914, 1:5-7; *El País,* April 26, 1914, 2:1.

the units ashore. As their boats neared the pier, they received rifle fire, thought to have come from the vicinity of the naval school or the public market. Three American picket launches, armed with one-pound guns, steamed at full speed along the waterfront near the navy school to try to locate the source of the firing. They dropped their shells into the school building until their fire was returned. *Prairie* then opened up with its three-inch guns at the windows, putting an end to all resistance there. Inside the building, a handful of cadets, all in their teens, crouched behind mattresses and furniture which they had pushed up against the windows for protection from the American guns. Before the students could be evacuated, one cadet was killed, sixteen-year-old Virgilio Uribe. Later in the afternoon the boys, with their commandant, Commodore Manuel Azueta, joined General Maass in Tejería.[26]

Both Fletcher and Canada made several attempts during the afternoon to find Maass or some public official in Veracruz in order to secure an armistice. Maass had no intention of returning from Tejería, and his men were diligently ripping up the railroad tracks between Tejería and Veracruz to stop any possible American drive on Mexico City. When it was evident that Maass was not in the city, Canada sent a messenger to the home of the mayor. Despite much pounding on the front door, the servants would not answer. The messenger then scaled the roof of the house and entered by way of the patio. He found the mayor cowering behind a barricade in his bathroom. The messenger gave him Admiral Fletcher's plea to stop the fighting in the city, but the mayor replied that he had no jurisdiction in the matter, that the chief of police should be found. The police station was deserted, however, so that the Americans could locate no one to assume authority. For the rest of the after-

[26] Canada, "Report"; Fletcher to Badger, "Report"; Maass to Secretaría de Guerra y Marina, April 22, 1914.

noon there was sporadic firing, though the American troops made no effort to advance beyond the positions they had taken in the morning. Fletcher still hoped he might avoid further bloodshed by means of negotiations with the Mexicans.[27]

At 1:30 p.m., while the firing ashore was most intense, *Ypiranga* arrived at Veracruz. She was hailed by *Utah* and ordered to stop outside the harbor, and an American officer went aboard to explain what was happening in the city. The German captain showed the bills of lading which proved that the arms for Huerta were aboard. They also showed, though the American government had not been aware of the fact, that the point of origin for the arms shipment had been New York, not Hamburg. Huerta's agents, to evade the American embargo, had purchased the weapons and ammunition from Remington and had had them shipped first to Germany as subterfuge. *Ypiranga's* captain was told that he might anchor in the inner harbor if he wished, but that he would not be allowed to leave the port without unloading the arms. He replied that he preferred to stay outside the harbor and would remain at anchor unless a storm should develop. He promised he would keep his ship within gun's reach of *Utah*.[28]

When the news of Fletcher's action reached Washington later the same day, Bryan called upon the German ambassador, J. H. von Bernstorff, to offer his government's apologies. He said that Fletcher, "through a misunderstanding," had exceeded his instructions. While the United States hoped that the munitions would be landed at Veracruz, said Bryan, so that they could be detained, his government did not claim the right—since there was no state of war—to interfere with *Ypiranga's* departure. Fletcher

27 Canada, "Report"; Fletcher to Badger, "Report."
28 Fletcher to Badger, "Report"; Canada to Bryan, April 21, 1914 /11595.

would be instructed to carry his apologies to the ship's captain. Thereafter there was little concern in Washington for *Ypiranga* or its cargo, even though it had been the instance for the seizure of Veracruz. As with the incident at Tampico, so it was with the arms shipment: One day's international crisis seemed conveniently forgotten on the morrow.[29]

Nightfall in Veracruz found the Americans still receiving occasional and scattered gunfire from various parts of the city. Most of the prisoners from "La Galera" had stayed behind as Contreras and Rodríguez Cerrillo retired, and now they roamed the streets, Winchester rifles slung over their shoulders, their pockets crammed with ammunition, discharging their weapons and looting stores and warehouses. The Americans returned the fire, and the three-inch guns on *Prairie* were used against any concentration of enemy shooting. Throughout the night the ships in the inner harbor played their searchlights on the city to aid their men ashore, and the American troops in the power station kept the street lights burning to prevent sniping. At 8:35 p.m., *San Francisco* arrived from Tampico and anchored in the inner harbor near *Prairie*. Her captain, C. T. Vogelsang, sent a landing party ashore immediately to join the men of the other ships. Shortly after midnight, *Chester's* captain, Commander Moffett, brought his vessel inside the harbor through the narrow, pitch-black entrance. At full speed and without the benefit of harbor lights, it was an effective feat of navigation. At 3 a.m. two companies of marines and *Chester's* company of seamen were put ashore. Slowly Fletcher's fighting force, which had been too small to effect the occupation of Veracruz, was being augmented. In the hours before dawn the buildup of forces continued, as the great ships of the Atlantic Fleet

[29] Bryan, "Memorandum," April 21, 1914 /17170.

put into port to discharge their men, followed by *Minnesota* and the transport *Hancock* from Tampico.[30]

Admiral Fletcher courteously offered to relinquish his command to Admiral Badger, but Badger requested him to keep charge of the occupation. As the new day began, Fletcher could face the military situation with more assurance. By the time *Minnesota* and *Hancock* had sent their contingents ashore, there were more than three thousand troops in Veracruz. Fletcher would have been even more comforted had he known that all of the soldiers of Maass were out of the city.[31]

Again on the morning of the twenty-second, Fletcher made a determined effort to find some of the Mexican officials in the city, but to no avail. It was clear now that the Mexican resistance was not organized, but, on the other hand, he could not permit it to go on with the consequent additional loss of life. Since there was now no government in Veracruz which could stop the firing, Fletcher, at 8 a.m., gave his commanders ashore the order to advance at their discretion. They were to suppress all desultory firing, taking possession of the entire city and restoring order. Marines moved down all the streets north of Independencia until they met with heavy and sustained fire from riflemen within the houses and atop hotels and other buildings. With characteristic precision the leathernecks then moved through the blocks, house by house, hacking their way through the adobe walls and clearing each building before entering the next. It was this efficient ruthlessness which caused many of the civilian casualties and the destruction of property. The battle-toughened marines, many of whom had seen action in the Philippines, were

[30] Canada, "Report"; Fletcher to Badger, "Report"; *Chester* Log, April 22, 1914; *Prairie* Log, April 22, 1914; Thomas, *Gimlet Eye*, 178; *Florida* Log, April 22, 1914; Canada to Bryan, April 22, 1914 /11599.

[31] Badger to Daniels, April 29, 1914, Daniels Papers, Box 35.

no respecters of person or estate as they accomplished their mission. Admiral Badger later wrote his approval to Secretary of the Navy Daniels: "I rather think that as increasing numbers of our men were killed or wounded, that eventually it fared rather badly with those discovered with arms in hand on the spot from which shooting came."[32]

While the marines mopped up resistance inside the city, the Second Regiment of seamen, formed from the crews of the battleships *New Hampshire, South Carolina,* and *Vermont,* advanced along the waterfront to protect the American left flank. As they crossed the open ground of the Benito Juárez park before the naval school—from which there had been firing the previous day—they marched in close order and at port arms. Though these sailors had never been under fire before, it showed a rare stupidity scarcely credible in the circumstances. They were a most inviting target. Suddenly, from the windows of the school building came the crack of a rifle shot, and then several more, and a number of bluejackets fell wounded or dead. The regiment quickly broke into firing positions and set up a fusillade of fire at the pock-marked facade of the school. At the same time, their commander, Captain Edwin A. Anderson of *New Hampshire,* signaled for support from the ships in the harbor. For several minutes *Prairie, Chester,* and *San Francisco,* all lying broadside to the naval school and at close range, poured heavy shells into the building. The firing soon ceased, and the Americans moved on into the southern part of the city.[33]

No one can say today who fired those shots at the Americans, whether some cadets who had remained in the school when the corps went to Tejería, a handful of civilians, or some of the men from "La Galera." This much is

[32] Badger to Daniels, April 29, 1914, Daniels Papers, Box 35; Canada, "Report"; Fletcher to Badger, "Report."
[33] Fletcher to Badger, "Report"; *Chester* Log, April 22, 1914.

certain—they were very few, else the loss of life in the ranks of the sailors would certainly have been higher. Even the poorest of marksmen could hardly have missed at that distance. This second shelling of the naval school virtually destroyed the inside of the building. Jack London, writing for *Collier's Magazine*, described the incident: "Had the taxpayer at home witnessed the way those upper story windows were put out by the *Chester's* shells, he would never again grudge the money spent of recent years in target practice. Onlookers say it reminded them of Buffalo Bill's exhibitions of rare shooting." For his work, Commander Moffett received the Congressional Medal of Honor.[34]

By 11 a.m. the city was completely in American hands. There was some sniping in the afternoon, and thereafter for a few days some isolated shots were heard, but the troops continued to make a house-to-house search for weapons and snipers, and it was possible to pass through the streets with comparative ease. Outposts were thrown out beyond the city in the surrounding sandhills to protect the occupation forces, while a marine guard took charge of the water pumping station at El Tejar which served Veracruz. All day, as ships arrived in the harbor, Fletcher landed troops, until by evening there were more than six thousand marines or bluejackets ashore to begin the gigantic task of repairing and cleaning up the city. The streets and plazas of Veracruz were littered with debris from the shelling. Various buildings were in shambles, either from shellfire or from looting by Mexicans and Americans. Bodies of fallen Mexicans lay in the streets as embarrassing reminders to the Americans of the high price of their occupation. In the tropical humidity of Veracruz, putrefaction set in

[34] Jack London, "With Funston's Men," *Collier's Magazine*, LIII (May 23, 1914), 9; Edward Arpee, *From Frigate to Flat-tops* (Lake Forest, Illinois, 1953), 46-48.

quickly, and scores of dogs and hundreds of vultures had to be driven away from each corpse. Since none of the Veracruzanos wished or dared to venture forth from their homes to take care of their own dead, the unwelcome task fell to the American marines and sailors. They buried some, but disposing of the bodies was both a difficult and noisome task. The simplest expedient was to drag the dead into large mounds, douse them liberally with crude petroleum, and set them afire. This was done in most instances.[35]

Because of this irregular means of handling the situation, no accurate count was ever made of Mexican casualties. But it is certain that at least two hundred died, and possibly more, as a result of American fire, while another three hundred were wounded. The American casualty figures, on the other hand, were surprisingly low: nineteen dead and forty-seven wounded. Since neither Contreras nor Rodríguez Cerrillo offered more than rearguard resistance and withdrew after losing but a few men, and the subsequent opposition was haphazard and ineffective, it must be assumed that most of the Mexicans killed or wounded were noncombatant civilians.

As hostilities ended, Canada published a plea for all shops and hotels to open their doors and to resume business as usual under the Americans. Most of the hotels and cantinas did so, but the other business establishments in the city were slower to comply. Their proprietors preferred to keep their iron fronts down until peace was assured. That evening, Admiral Fletcher issued a proclamation to the people of Veracruz stating that his forces had "temporarily" occupied their city "to supervise the administration of affairs on account of the present disturbed conditions in Mexico." He made no mention of the Tampico incident or

[35] Fletcher to Badger, "Report"; Canada, "Report." Canada's report has photographs of the American troops burning the bodies.

of any retaliatory action taken by the United States. Again he invited all public officials to resume their duties. Fletcher promised that the military authorities would not interfere so long as peace and good order were maintained.[36]

For four days Fletcher sought without success to persuade the federal, state, and city officials in Veracruz to take charge of their own government. At the same time he threatened to impose martial law if the sniping against his troops was not halted. The state and federal functionaries said frankly that they could not serve under an invading force and pointed out to Fletcher the punishment provided under national law for such an action. On April 24, the city council met to consider the question. Robert J. Kerr, an American lawyer long resident in Mexico, appeared at the meeting to state the case for the Americans and to urge the councilmen, for their own protection, to cooperate with the military forces. The local officials at first promised to resume direction of the city's affairs. But since so many offices in Veracruz had been under the control of the state and national governments, and the nocturnal shooting continued, Fletcher found it imperative to proclaim full military control of the city. On April 26, after a conference with the mayor, he decreed martial law for Veracruz. At the same time he began planning to turn over the occupation of the city to the American army.[37]

In the critical days before the landing at Veracruz, many in the United States, particularly Republican leaders, had urged Woodrow Wilson to call upon the army for service in Mexico. In his cabinet, Secretary of War Lindley M. Garrison stood most strongly for full-scale intervention. Wilson turned a deaf ear to these opinions, believing that the occupation could be carried out without incident and

[36] Canada, "Report"; Canada to Bryan, April 22, 1914 /11602; *La Opinión* (Veracruz), April 23, 1914, 1:3-5.
[37] Fletcher to Badger, "Report"; Canada, "Report."

bloodlessly. With the resistance of the Mexicans, however, he was forced, most reluctantly, on April 23 to order an infantry brigade under the command of General Frederick Funston to Veracruz. Admiral Fletcher, too, preferred, if the occupation would be of long duration, to see the army in charge of the city. In short order, Funston assembled his forces at Galveston, Texas, where they went aboard waiting transports. By the evening of the twenty-seventh, they were in the harbor of Veracruz, ready to go ashore to relieve the marines and sailors.[38]

On the following morning, Funston and Fletcher conferred on the best means of effecting a change in the administration procedures in Veracruz, and they agreed to appoint a civilian as governor of the occupied territory. Fletcher had been impressed by the qualifications of Robert J. Kerr, and so, without consulting Washington, the two decided to offer the post to him. Two other Americans in Veracruz, William F. Buckley and Charles H. Stewart, were to assist Kerr, while a navy officer, Commander H. O. Stickney, was named inspector of the port, in charge of collecting import and export revenues. Buckley, like Kerr, was a lawyer who had business interests in Mexico and had been closely associated with the government of Victoriano Huerta. The choice of Kerr by Fletcher and Funston was purely fortuitous, since they knew nothing of his background, but it was an unfortunate blunder, nonetheless. Kerr had only recently returned from the United States, where he had given a number of public lectures highly critical of Woodrow Wilson. He had told his audiences that Wilson's policy in Mexico was that of the Standard Oil Company, and that the American government showed no concern for the rights of its citizens there. The

[38] *New York Herald,* April 24, 1914, 1:7-8; Fletcher to Daniels, April 22, 1914 /11578.

Mexicans, he said, were fit only for a "beneficent depo-tism" such as that of Porfirio Díaz.[39]

It was impossible for Washington to support this ap-pointment. In the United States there were strong protests on the part of the Democrats, who charged that only Re-publicans were being chosen to work with the military government in Veracruz. Though Funston wrote testily to the secretary of war that neither he nor Kerr had "taken into consideration any man's political belief," and that they cared "just as much about a man's politics as we do about the color of his hair," Garrison announced to the press on May 1 that Kerr would be replaced by an army officer. In his reply to Funston, Garrison stressed that it was "un-wise to place an American civilian in charge" in Veracruz. He and the president preferred that the Mexicans run their own affairs, if possible, and that otherwise the gov-ernment should be completely military in character.[40]

For two days the soldiers stayed aboard their transports in the harbor while General Funston and Admiral Fletcher worked out the details for the transfer of authority from the navy to the army. The marine battalions proved to be a bone of contention, however, and there soon developed an interservice pulling and hauling for their control. There were now more than three thousand leathernecks in Vera-cruz, and Badger recommended to Josephus Daniels that they be left ashore under Fletcher's direction. If this was not possible, he said, he preferred that they be withdrawn

[39] *La Opinión* (Veracruz), April 29, 1914, 4:1-2; Martin J. Hutchens to Bryan, April 29, 1914, State Department Files, National Archives, Wilson-Bryan Correspondence, Vol. II; Napoleon Hill to Wilson, April 29, 1914 /11863; *New York Times*, April 30, 1914, 2:7; Robert J. Kerr, "American Citizens in Foreign Countries," *Annals of the American Academy of Political and Social Science*, LIV (July, 1914), 236-242.

[40] Funston to Agwar (Adjutant General, War Department), May 1, 1914 /11811; Lindley M. Garrison to Funston, May 1, 1914, Army Files, National Archives, AGO Files, Roller Drawer 6 (hereafter cited as RD 6); *New York Herald*, May 3, 1914, 1:3-5; *New York Times*, May 2, 1914, 1:7.

to the ships. The army, on the other hand, asked for a uni-
fied command in Veracruz, with all troops under General
Funston. The matter was ultimately carried to a cabinet
meeting in Washington, where Daniels and Garrison argued
the cases for their respective services. In the end, Wilson
decided in favor of the army. He ordered the marines
detached from the Atlantic Fleet and detailed for service
with the army for the duration of the occupation. Thereafter, Funston had complete charge of the forces in Veracruz. On April 30 the army brigade was disembarked and
paraded through the streets of the city. They were to remain in Mexico much longer than anyone expected.[41]

The news of the landing at Veracruz caught most Mexicans by surprise. Despite rumors and occasional hints in
the newspapers of the trouble between the United States
and Mexico, the censorship exercised by Huerta's government had kept the public in ignorance of the true state of
affairs. Because it came so suddenly and without warning,
the occupation seemed nothing less than naked aggression
against their country. The newspapers in Mexico City now
vied in publishing the most scurrilous and inflammatory
attacks on the United States and Woodrow Wilson. On
April 21, *El Imparcial* headlined: "The soil of the *patria* is
defiled by foreign invasion! We may die, but let us kill!"
Two days later, *El Independiente* cried: "While Mexicans
were massacring the gringo pigs, the church bells rang out
their glory!" *La Patria,* in a bold banner across the front
page, called for "Vengeance! Vengeance! Vengeance!" And
again on the twenty-fourth the editors of *El Imparcial*
reviled the "pigs of *Yanquilandia.*" All of the Mexican
newspapers carried reports that General Joaquín Maass,

---

[41] Chief of Staff to AGO, April 26, 1914, AGO Files, RG 94, Box 7474;
Badger to Daniels, April 26, 1914, Navy File 27741/1014; Garrison to
Wilson, April 26, 1914, AGO Files, RG 94, Box 7474; Daniels to Badger,
April 27, 1914, Navy File 27741/1023.

brother of the federal commander at Veracruz, would soon lead an army of twenty thousand Mexicans into Texas to avenge the American attack. Official government publications sounded the call to arms: The Mexican people must combat the invaders.[42]

Throughout Mexico the public responded with vehemence to the intemperate language of the periodicals, as throngs rioted against American consulates or businesses. In Mexico City, while government employees and school children marched through the streets chanting "Death to the Gringos!" a mob wrenched loose a statue of George Washington from its base in a plaza and substituted a small bust of their own hero of independence, Father Miguel Hidalgo. A group of unruly boys broke the glass doors of the consulate and carried off the coat of arms which had hung over the entrance. In the center of the capital, windows were shattered in the American Club, in the American Photo Supply Company, and in Sanborn's Drugstore, and the office of the *Mexican Herald* was stoned. The Porter Hotel was invaded by a lawless band who shouted insults at the guests and smashed the hotel's windows. Agitators roused crowds to repeated acts of violence against the Americans, and for several days American shops and businesses remained closed as angry demonstrations continued in the streets. Fearful of the unleashed national passions, Nelson O'Shaughnessy collected arms and ammunition to permit the members of the American colony to defend themselves against attack. But when the initial fury had run its course, the governor of the Federal District, Eduardo Iturbide, gave the Americans ample protection, so that there were no injuries except to properties.[43]

[42] *El Imparcial,* April 21, 1914; *El Independiente,* April 23, 1914; *La Patria,* April 23, 1914; *El Imparcial,* April 24, 1914, 3:3-4; *Periódico Oficial de Veracruz,* April 21, 1914, 1:1.
[43] Canada to Bryan, April 23, 1914 /11652, April 24, 1914 /11689, and April 25, 1914 /11720.

The official Mexican reaction was immediate and decisive, as Huerta's government broke off diplomatic relations between the two countries. On April 22, Nelson O'Shaughnessy was handed his passports and asked to leave Mexico. For O'Shaughnessy, this was virtually the end of his diplomatic career. Wilson would not give him another position commensurate with his experience and abilities, and, after a brief and unimportant mission in Austria, he was dropped from the Foreign Service. In Mexico City, after the expulsion of O'Shaughnessy, American affairs were handled by the Brazilian minister, J. M. Cardoso de Oliveira.[44]

Outside the capital there were other anti-American demonstrations in areas still under control of Huerta's government. At Progreso and Mazatlán, doors and windows were smashed and American residences were ransacked. At Mazatlán the consulate was stoned by an angry crowd shouting threats at the Americans. The mob was dispersed by mounted police, and the governor of Sinaloa made a formal apology to the consul, William E. Alger. Alger, with the precedent of the Tampico affair behind him, took a strong position, informing the federal authorities that a repetition of the "outrage" would compel the United States to take measures to "insure respect." What might have become an international incident with serious consequences occurred in Monterrey when a group of citizens, led by a federal officer, attacked the American consulate, tore down the flags displayed there, trampled on them, and then burned them. And worse, the consul, William C. Hanna, was taken prisoner by Huerta's officers, charged with being too friendly with the Constitutionalists. Hanna was released within a day when the federal garrison abandoned the city to the rebels, but it is worth noting that the American government took no notice of these incidents, which were

[44] O'Shaughnessy to Bryan, April 22, 1914, State Department Files, 123, Os4/122.

patently much more grave than the events which had inspired the occupation of Veracruz.[45]

In Tampico the situation was complicated by the original incident there and by the continued presence of the armed American vessels at the mouth of the Pánuco River. There was every indication that the landing and occupation of Veracruz would be followed by similar action at Tampico. Late on the afternoon of April 21, as news reached Tampico of the seizure of Veracruz, Morelos Zaragoza published a call to the citizens of Tamaulipas to resist with force any invasion there. Within an hour, crowds began to assemble in the central plaza to hear impassioned orators inciting the Mexicans to violence. Morelos Zaragoza made no attempt to curb the speeches or the disorders which followed. A brick was thrown through a hotel window, Sanborn's Restaurant was stoned, and the glass door of the American consulate was broken. The demonstrations were largely vocal, however. The rioting continued until after midnight with little real damage and no loss of life or injury to the Americans in the city.[46]

As the violence began, Clarence Miller tried to communicate with Mayo to ask for protection. There was no direct means of reaching Mayo, since all of the American warships were now outside the river, though Miller was able to arrange for the radio operator of the yacht *Wakiva* to relay messages telephoned to the Huasteca Oil Company dock from the consulate. Miller told Mayo of the rioting in the city—which seemed at the time much worse than it actually was—and asked for assistance. The radio operator on *Wakiva* added his own opinion that all of the Americans in Tampico were in danger of being killed. Mayo replied

---

45 William E. Alger to Bryan, April 24, 1914 /11697; William C. Hanna to Bryan, April 24, 1914 /11719.
46 "Bulletin No. 21," April 21, 1914, RG 45/659; "Events in Tampico," RG 45/659.

that he could not bring his ships back into the river without worsening the situation. Suddenly, as *Minnesota* was receiving a new message from Miller, *Wakiva's* radio went dead. Federal officers on the Mexican gunboat *Zaragoza* had intercepted the messages and put in at the Huasteca dock to cut the telephone wire. At the same time they ordered the radio operator to stop his transmissions. Mayo could not know this. The ominous silence of *Wakiva* seemed to imply trouble ashore, and the American admiral could only believe the worst.[47]

Mayo decided to enter the river, if necessary by force, to bring out the American refugees. He asked Captain H. M. Doughty of the British cruiser *Hermione* to inform Morelos Zaragoza that the warships were coming to Tampico solely for that purpose and that he hoped nothing would occur to interfere with the "peaceful nature of their mission." Doughty feared that this action might be interpreted in Tampico as the beginning of landing operations, and he told Mayo that he thought it best that the American ships remain outside. He promised he would see that the refugees were escorted out safely. Mayo quickly agreed, and the British commander, aided by German officers on the cruiser *Dresden*, took charge of all of the private vessels in the river, running up British and German flags to assure their neutrality. Ships large and small shuttled back and forth for several hours, until all who wished to leave could do so. Clarence Miller toured the city up to the last minute, making certain that all Americans were out of Tampico, and then he too went aboard a British vessel.[48]

The American civilians were completely in the dark concerning the plans of the navy. They knew only that the

[47] Miller, "Political Conditions"; Mayo to Fletcher, April 23, 1914, RG 45/659.

[48] H. M. Doughty to Mayo, April 23, 1914, RG 45/659; *Des Moines* Log, April 23, 1914; *Dolphin* Log, April 23, 1914.

seizure of Tampico had been imminent when Huerta refused to comply with Mayo's demands. They now believed that a state of war existed with Mexico, and that they had been brought out temporarily so that the navy could attack the city. Within a day or two, they hoped, they could safely return to their homes. They were unpleasantly surprised, therefore, to learn that they would be taken to the United States. Many had come aboard the ships with no money and only the clothing they wore. Most had homes or businesses which would now be left behind unprotected. Moreover, there were many small children and infants in the group, and now all were herded into cramped and uncomfortable quarters on the warships. They protested vigorously to Mayo, demanding that they be allowed to return to Tampico. The admiral was adamant and would not risk going into the river again. He sent them all on to Galveston.[49]

After spending several days in quarantine before they were permitted to land, the refugees were met by government officials and given quarters in the hotels of Galveston. Those without funds were furnished transportation to their homes in the United States. But they refused to be mollified and remained bitterly critical of the American government. Many signed mass letters of protest against their treatment or sent telegrams to members of Congress.[50]

To counter the angry criticism which added fuel to the Republican attacks against the administration, Josephus Daniels gave a statement to the press placing the responsibility on Admiral Mayo. He said that Mayo had made

[49] Victor Blue, "The Tampico Incident," April (?), 1914, Daniels Papers, Box 373; Miller, "Political Conditions"; Mayo to Badger, April 23, 1914, RG 45/653, and April 30, 1914, RG 45/659.

[50] *New York Times*, April 29, 1914, 3:2-5, and April 30, 1914, 3:1; "Statement of Facts given the People of the United States by 372 Refugees," April (?), 1914, RG 45/157; J. B. Wood to A. B. Fall, April 28, 1914, Bryan Papers, Library of Congress, Box 38.

the decision to withdraw the ships from the river in order to avoid trouble at Tampico. This patently inaccurate statement by the secretary of the navy brought strong letters of protest from both Mayo and Badger. But the misstatement (or lack of information) on the part of Daniels was characteristic of the government's muddling through the crisis without a clear-cut policy or effective leadership. As the United States moved on to the next phase of its relations with Mexico, neither the president nor his cabinet seemed disturbed that their actions had caused a large number of Americans to be uprooted from their homes and properties and brought to the United States against their will. Wilson believed, evidently, that most had gone to Mexico to exploit the Mexican people. In the end, most were able to make their way back to Tampico after the city was taken by the Constitutionalists in May, but not without great inconvenience, expense, and hardship.[51]

In the United States the public gave its approval to the use of force at Veracruz as it had to the earlier threats of Woodrow Wilson. Most citizens agreed with their president that the American flag had been insulted and that military action was a fit reward for the Mexicans responsible. Newspapers of all hues supported Wilson, though those affiliated with the Republican party grew instantly critical when it became apparent that the American troops were not going on to Mexico City. They lampooned Wilson's professed policy of "watchful waiting," and spoke bitingly of Wilson's "Hesitation Waltz"—"One step forward, two steps backward, and then sidestep." Wilson was unmoved by such criticism. His hope now was that the Mexicans themselves could be persuaded—not forced—to see the error of their ways, that they would reasonably and spontaneously

[51] *New York Times,* May 8, 1914, 2:1; Badger to Daniels, "Report on the withdrawal of the U. S. Naval ships from Pánuco River," May 9, 1914, Daniels Papers, Box 255.

agree to stop the useless civil war, that free elections would be held to choose a successor for Huerta, genuinely representative of the Mexican people.[52]

The news from Veracruz that Mexican soldiers had resisted the landing came as a rude shock to Woodrow Wilson. He had been convinced that there would be no opposition, for to resist such overwhelming force was not "sensible." John Lind and others had assured him that the seizure of the city would be a "gesture involving little or no danger." If Wilson was obstinate, he was also compassionate. He was deeply moved and disturbed, therefore, by the reports of casualties on both sides. As Wilson called reporters together in the White House to announce the deaths of the sailors and marines, he appeared "pale, parchmenty," and "positively shaken."[53]

It was not an auspicious time for the president in either his personal or public life. Mrs. Wilson did not seem to respond to the medical treatment of Dr. Grayson or the rest cure at White Sulphur Springs. Though Wilson professed to be optimistic about the state of her health, it was apparent that she was not improving. He was also disturbed, more than he would have admitted, by the approaching marriage of his daughter Eleanor to McAdoo. Dr. Grayson told House that the president did not "want her to leave him." House was in New York formulating plans to keep the peace in Europe. Now Grayson asked him to return to Washington for a few days, for "our friend needs you at this particular time." Wilson seemed to retreat more and more into himself, not discussing even important issues with the members of his cabinet. The attorney general, Thomas W. Gregory, complained to House that he knew nothing about the president's decisions until he "saw it in the news-

---

[52] *Literary Digest*, XLVIII (May 2, 1914), 1029-1032; *New York World*, April 23, 1914, 3:1-2.
[53] Baker Chronological Files, Box 63, April 21, 1914.

papers." No longer did Wilson concern himself with threats and retaliations. Instead, the punitive expedition became a testament of brotherly love of the United States toward the people of Mexico.[54]

Wilson took the opportunity of the public funeral for the men killed at Veracruz to make public his new attitudes. On May 11 he journeyed to New York with Colonel House to deliver an address at the Brooklyn Navy Yard. As usual, he had not prepared his speech beforehand, though he had made "mental notes" as he drove out to the yard. Yet he spoke movingly and with conviction about the mission of the United States. "We have gone down to Mexico to serve mankind, if we can find out the way," he said. He prayed that those now being honored, those who had bravely offered their lives at Veracruz, had not done so in vain.[55]

Back in the White House, Wilson expressed similar sentiments to Samuel G. Blythe, who was preparing an atricle about the president for the *Saturday Evening Post*. He declared that his sole object in Mexico was "to help the people secure the liberty" which was fully theirs by right. This liberty could never be won, he said, while Huerta remained in power. The forces of the United States would stay in Mexico until Huerta either resigned or was eliminated.[56]

Wilson believed that the revolutionaries in Mexico would welcome the overt American assistance. In this, Wilson erred, for General Carranza was fully as obdurate as the American president about what he knew to be right, and the first chief would not believe that Wilson knew what was best for the Mexican people. Undoubtedly the Constitutionalists would find it easier to defeat Huerta with the

[54] House Diary, April 14, 1914; Cary T. Grayson to House, April 26, 1914, House Papers; House Diary, April 26, 1914.
[55] House Diary, May 11, 1914; *New York Times*, May 12, 1914, 3:3-5.
[56] Samuel G. Blythe, "Mexico: The Record of a Conversation with President Wilson," *Saturday Evening Post*, CLXXXVI (May 23, 1914), 2-4.

Americans in control of Veracruz, shutting off the government's source of arms, but they would not accept aid if it meant intervention in Mexico's affairs. Carranza was worthy flint for Wilson's steel, and between these two strong personalities there was to be trouble for over a year. In the end the first chief won out. He would not be moved by Wilson to do anything he did not want to do.

On the evening of April 21, twelve hours after the forces of Admiral Fletcher had gone ashore at Veracruz, Bryan telegraphed George Carothers, a special agent for the State Department in Mexico, asking him to see Carranza "to make known to him the President's position." The United States felt itself justified in using its armed forces, he said, "to compel redress for a specific indignity." But Wilson was always careful, said the secretary of state, "to distinguish between General Huerta and his supporters on one side, and the rest of the Mexican people on the other." The president reiterated his friendship for the people of Mexico and hoped that the Constitutionalists would not "misconstrue his acts." In reply, Carranza penned a characteristically long and rambling recitation of Huerta's crimes. The individual acts of Victoriano Huerta, he wrote, would "never be sufficient to involve the Mexican nation in a disastrous war with the United States." Rather than accept the tacit alliance with the American forces, he denounced the "invasion of our territory and the permanency of your forces in the port of Veracruz." He invited the government of the United States to "suspend the hostile acts already initiated, ordering your forces to evacuate [the city]."[57]

In contrast to the truculent attitude of Venustiano Carranza, Francisco Villa was openly conciliatory. His antagonism toward the first chief was growing daily, as

[57] Bryan to George C. Carothers, April 21, 1914 /11608a; Carothers to Bryan, April 22, 1914 /11618; *New York Times*, April 23, 1914, 1:6-7.

Carranza sought to minimize his efforts as a revolutionary leader and to prevent his reaching Mexico City before Obregón, González, or the other Constitutionalist commanders. He was pleased to seize this opportunity to demonstrate his independence and to drive a wedge between Carranza and the American government. On April 23, Villa expressed to Carothers his warm friendship for the United States. So far as he was concerned, he said, the Americans could "keep Veracruz and hold it so tight that not even water could get in to Huerta!" Villa told a reporter for the *New York Times* that his men wished "only the closest and most friendly relations with our neighbors to the north." Bryan was delighted with Villa's response. To the secretary of state he was a "high-minded and noble citizen." Naively he wrote to Carothers that Villa showed a "comprehension of the whole situation that is greatly to his credit."[58]

Villa's affability was not shared, however, elsewhere in the Constitutionalist camp. All of the principal chiefs rallied to support Carranza. Though Obregón rebuffed the invitation of a federal commander to join forces against the Americans, he announced ominously that his own troops would "fight the invaders until they have exhausted every effort to resist."[59]

The initial reaction in most quarters was that the American invasion meant war between the two countries. If war was avoided and the hostilities limited to Veracruz, it was because calmer counsels prevailed on both sides. The American forces in Veracruz were given strict orders to stay there and to refrain from any hostile action against the Mexican army. Huerta, too, when it was abundantly

---

[58] Carothers to Bryan, April 23, 1914 /11654; *New York Times*, April 24, 1914, 1:3; House Diary, May 8, 1914; Bryan to Carothers, April 24, 1914 /11654.
[59] Louis Hostetler to Bryan, April 24, 1914 /11668.

clear that the Constitutionalists would not unite with him against the Americans, followed a more peaceful course. Yet both Huerta and Wilson were proud men, disinclined to make the first step toward reconciliation. As the two nations hovered between peace and war, the principal countries of Latin America gave both presidents the opportunity to end the impasse with honor. The ministers of Argentina, Brazil, and Chile in Washington joined on April 24 in offering to mediate the dispute. They also invited Carranza and the Constitutionalists to enter into discussions to bring peace to Mexico.[60]

The mediation attempt resembled nothing so much as an elaborate quadrille from *Alice in Wonderland* in which nothing anyone did or said made sense to anyone else. Carranza accepted the invitation "in principle" and then refused to send delegates to the conference because he would not recognize the right of outsiders to intermeddle in Mexican affairs. Huerta's government accepted, believing that the conference would deal with the quarrel between the United States and Mexico. Woodrow Wilson readily assented to the mediation, but insisted that the United States was not a party to it. The conference, he said, would be limited to the internal Mexican situation, to an attempt to find a regime in Mexico satisfactory to all factions. Given the extreme intransigence on all sides, the mediation had little chance of success.[61]

Robert Lansing prepared a memorandum for Wilson to guide the American government in its relations with the mediators. Artfully jesuitical, Lansing found that the real quarrel of the United States was with conditions in Mexico, not with any faction there. And since this was the case, he said, the mediators and the representatives from Mexico could meet on American (hence neutral) soil. Accepting

[60] "Circular Telegram," May 2, 1914 /11802a.
[61] *Periódico Oficial de Veracruz*, June 25, 1914, 1-12.

the reasoning of the State Department counselor, Wilson designated commissioners who would be *near*, not *at*, the mediation conference. It was a fine distinction, but one which undoubtedly pleased the president, for he drew it throughout the conference. Huerta, believing that his dispute was with the American government, insisted that the conference be held outside the United States, and the mediators readily agreed to meet at the Canadian Niagara Falls. As late as May 21, when the first session was held in the sun parlor of Niagara Falls' Clifton House, however, the A.B.C. ministers believed that they were presiding over a mediation between Huerta and the United States.[62]

For more than a month the mediators sought to find a formula for the solution to Mexico's problems which would satisfy both Huerta and Carranza, as well as the United States. It proved to be an impossible task. Huerta's delegates opposed the naming of a revolutionary as provisional president, while the Constitutionalists—observing from afar—refused even to hear of a negotiated peace with the Huertista regime, much less an election in which the followers of Huerta would participate. At the end of June, 1914, as the mediators recessed indefinitely, it was apparent that the conference had accomplished nothing. The American forces were still in Veracruz, and there seemed no immediate way to get them out. Wilson would not consider evacuating the city until Huerta resigned the presidency. Huerta, on the other hand, could not be eliminated until the armies of Carranza reached Mexico City. The answer to the problem lay on the battlefields of Mexico, and in the military prowess of Alvaro Obregón, Pablo González, and Francisco Villa. There were battles to be fought, men to be killed, towns to be seized. In the meantime, for

[62] Robert Lansing, "Memorandum on Place of Conference of Mediators," May 1, 1914 /11800½; Domisio da Gama and others to Bryan, May 5, 1914 /11849.

the American marines and soldiers in Veracruz, it was to be a long, hot, and difficult summer.[63]

[63] Percival Dodge to Bryan, May 22, 1914 /12048, and May 23, 1914 /12070; Frank H. Severance, "The Peace Conference at Niagara Falls in 1914," *Buffalo Historical Society Publications,* XVIII (1914), 3-75. The University of Texas Latin American Collection has papers of William F. Buckley and Emilio Rabasa (one of Huerta's representatives) dealing with the mediation attempt.

FOUR

The Proconsuls

THE CHILD WAS scarcely a year old when he died of stomach cramps. Small for his age, he had suffered from diarrhea periodically since his birth, and because the family was poor, there had never been sufficient money to summon a doctor. Instead the mother had visited the herb woman and obtained a mysterious concoction said to cure stomach ailments. The herb woman had a thriving business, and her trays, carefully displayed in her allotted space outside the market, contained remedies for almost every affliction of mankind. In Veracruz among the poorer population there was much need for such remedies. When he knew that the child was dead, the father went to the coffinmaker to rent a small box for the occasion. He had been there before; he would go again, for death was no stranger in the thatched houses of Veracruz. For two pesos—and a small deposit—he obtained a roughhewn pine box, unpainted and with no lining of any kind, a few artificial flowers, and a cheap shroud. As he trotted home, barefooted, through the dusty stone streets, carefully balancing the tiny box on his head, no one seemed to care or to remark his passing. No one, that is, except for one American, the Red Cross representative, Charles Jenkinson, who described the funeral in an article for *Survey*. Jenkinson had come to Veracruz to help care for the indigent, the sick, and the dying. While the Americans held the city, the Red Cross paid for sixty-one funerals such as this.[1]

That night the family sat around the coffin, placed in the center of the earth floor of their hut, conversing, eating, and drinking. Two wax tapers, one on each side of the coffin, eerily illuminated the barren room. There were no tears, no sadness, only a profound resignation before God's inscrutable will. In a sense the child was fortunate. The "Little Angel" was already with God, the Holy Mother, and the Blessed Saints. Only life on earth, in the hot summer of Veracruz, was full of sorrow, discomfort, and hardship. No one slept during the night, for occasions such as this, when friends and family might gather together, must be savored and prolonged. Early the next morning the coffin was carried—again on the father's head—directly to the cemetery. An indigent family could ill afford the fee charged by the priests for a church funeral. Besides, if the child was in Heaven, what need was there for elaborate obsequies? At the cemetery a small grave, two feet deep, had already been prepared, and the year's rent of three pesos paid in advance. The child's body was rolled into the shallow hole and then buried without ceremony. The wooden coffin, the tawdry flowers, and the shroud were returned to the shop and the deposit left on the previous day recovered. If at any time the rent for the year were not paid by the family, the child's bones would be dug up and tossed into a large trench at one end of the cemetery. The burial plot was then rented again.

Sickness and death, like dirt and disorder, were accepted in Veracruz with equanimity. For each one thousand per-

[1] Jenkinson, "Veracruz," 133-141.

sons in the city, nearly fifty died every month; more than half of these were infants under a year old. They died of dysentery, of malaria, of tuberculosis, of meningitis, of smallpox. One of the first tasks of the American army, if the troops were to stay in Veracruz, was to reduce the incidence of disease and the high mortality rate, if only to protect the soldiers. This could be done only by a thorough cleanup of the city by the military government. No one in Washington had anticipated the magnitude of the problem involved in taking and holding Veracruz. It proved to be a feat worthy of Hercules.[2]

On April 30, 1914, the army's Fifth Brigade came ashore at Veracruz, and many believed (or hoped) that the men would continue marching until they reached Mexico City, that the three thousand soldiers in this contingent represented but a part of a larger expeditionary force which would pacify Mexico. Among these was their commander, Frederick Funston; his chief, Secretary of War Garrison; the Republicans in the United States; most of the American newspapers; and abroad, the American colony in Mexico and the government of Great Britain, which was disturbed because of the mistreatment of British nationals by revolutionaries such as Villa. The expectation that the landing of troops meant war brought to Veracruz a large number of special correspondents to report the hostilities. Some were famous, some were not; but they were all there to see battles. There was Richard Harding Davis, with a worldwide reputation for his description of fighting men in action, and the noted novelist, Jack London. There was Arthur Ruhl for *Collier's* and Frederick Palmer of *Everybody's Magazine*. The Associated Press, the United Press, and more than twenty-five American newspapers maintained representatives in the city. But Veracruz was as far as most of them got, for Woodrow Wilson was determined that there

[2] Jenkinson, "Veracruz," 133-141; London, "With Funston's Men," 11.

would be no war with Mexico. And so the soldiers and marines, 7,150 in all, remained in the port for the next seven months, through the hottest, most disagreeable time of the year.[3]

Once the occupation was complete and hostilities ended, Veracruz began to return to its normal life. The business establishments, the shops, the banks, which had all closed on April 21, were now opened again. The hotels were full, the restaurants and cantinas did a thriving trade, and once again the Veracruzanos could congregate in the plazas and at the tables under the giant fans of the Portales. Ships came and departed in the harbor, for there was no need for a blockade now that the Americans held the port facilities.[4]

If business was normal, there was much that was new. Great changes were taking place, and before the month of May was out, Veracruz was a different city, so altered as to be almost unrecognizable. This change—for better or for worse—was due to the American military government. For one thing, there was the presence in the city of thousands of foreign troops, and an occupational force, if it does not fight, must be kept busy, lest morale disintegrate. There were parades to be held, guards to be mounted, outposts to be manned, and the spit and polish of ordinary army and marine corps life everywhere. The impact of the troops on the city population was profound. When the buglers sounded "First Call" in the morning—and it was earlier and earlier as the hot season wore on—the people of Veracruz were awakened as well. There was money put into circulation, in good American dollars, spent in shops and cantinas and in the segregated district. On paydays the houses of the district did a thriving business, as long lines of soldiers or marines waited patiently for their brief mo-

[3] Funston, "Report of Operations, April 20–June 30, 1914," AGO Files, RD 6; *New York Herald*, April 20, 1914, 10:2-3; *Washington Post*, May 2, 1914, 6:2.
[4] London, "With Funston's Men," 9; Ruhl, "Unfinished Drama," 22.

ments of pleasure. There was no public gambling, for the military government closed the gaming houses, the cock-fighting arenas, and the bullring, and banished the sellers of lottery tickets. But there were other amusements, organized by the military commanders or the Red Cross—baseball, footraces, boxing, movies, and band concerts in the principal plazas.[5]

Despite the boasts from Mexico City that federal armies would soon drive the Americans out of Veracruz or that an attack would be made into the United States, no such retaliation materialized. There was only one minor clash between the Mexicans and Funston's troops near Veracruz. On May 2, a party of federal soldiers appeared at El Tejar, where marines guarded the water pumping station, to ask that the Americans turn over the control of the station to the Mexicans. When the demand was refused, the federals withdrew a short distance and fired upon the marines. The fire was returned, and the Mexicans were driven off. There were no casualties on either side. Thereafter, General Maass was content to keep his troops away from the American lines, though he did set up a blockade from the land side to keep food from reaching the city.[6]

At first the blockade was highly effective, and the flow of meats, vegetables, milk, and charcoal coming in from the hill country slowed to a trickle. It was only intermittently enforced, however, so that supplies did get through to the city. Yet food was always scarce, for the population of Veracruz had been greatly augmented by the American invasion. Not only were there the American troops to be fed, but an uncounted number of refugees passed through the port. Funston estimated that more than two thousand Mexicans sailed from Veracruz each month to escape the revolutionaries, while many more were forced to remain

[5] Davis, "When Is a War," 44; Jenkinson, "Veracruz," 133-141.

[6] Funston, "Report of Operations, July 1—November 26, 1914," AGO Files, RD 6 (hereafter cited as Funston, "Report").

in the city because they had no money or were unable to book passage on the commercial liners that called at Veracruz. With the shortages the prices of foodstuffs began to rise, and by the middle of June they were two or three times higher than they had been before the occupation. Hungry women and children watched the Americans at each meal and then eagerly fought for and devoured the scraps that were left. General Funston offered to "tear any blockade to bits in half an hour," but Garrison replied that there must be no hostilities unless he was attacked by the Mexicans. Food could be brought in by sea, if necessary, he said. Subsequently the port authorities permitted foods to be imported duty-free from the United States, but although this alleviated the situation, there was never enough for all while the Americans were in Veracruz.[7]

During the first week in May, Funston continued to hope for orders to proceed to Mexico City. In his dispatches to the War Department he stressed the danger to Americans if the army of Zapata should take the capital. He spoke ominously of "pillage" and "massacre." "Merely give the order," he said to Garrison, "and leave the rest to me." Garrison agreed completely, but his hands were tied by Wilson's avowed policy of peace. He told Funston again to make no advance, even if attacked, without consulting Washington.[8]

If the inactivity of the troops was vexing to their commanders, who had come to Mexico to fight, it was doubly so to the correspondents, such as Richard Harding Davis. He was like an old war stallion, champing at the bit, as he attempted to put color and glory and flagwaving into dispatches that told of mundane events. About the dis-

[7] *Mexican Herald,* May 2, 1:6-7, and June 13, 1914, 2:3; Funston to Agwar, May 1, 1914, AGO Files, RG 94, Box 7474; Garrison to Funston, May 2, 1914, AGO Files, RD 6; John B. Porter, "Orders No. 5, June 16, 1914," AGO File 2228507.

[8] Funston to Agwar, May 7, 1914, War Diary, AGO File 2228507, 14.

embarking of the army units, which he had witnessed, Davis wrote: "Veracruz felt that the foeman's boot was on her shore when six thousand hobnailed brogans struck the asphalt with the regularity of pile drivers. Except in bronze on their monuments the natives had never seen such supermen of such heroic aspect. . . . This morning they could have marched not only from the wharf to the plaza, but from the harbor to Mexico City." And of the landing of the marines and bluejackets before his arrival, he said: "Opposed by an enemy they could not see, in the streets of a strange city where every house was an ambush and where every church tower had a fighting top, with a smile in their eyes and slang on their lips, they tossed away their lives as carelessly as they would pump out an empty cartridge."[9]

Such flamboyant inaccuracy was characteristic of Davis, who wrote of battle without ever being a part of it. If war came to Mexico, it would be ugly, dirty, and hot. But Davis had brought his civilization with him to Mexico, his portable bathtub, his immaculate white linen suits, and his evening clothes, as well as his "war equipment." Each evening in Veracruz, as he sat down to dinner under the Portales, he wore a formal jacket. Though it was hot and muggy, Davis seemed as "fresh and clean as though he were in a New York or London restaurant." Vexed by the indolent life in Veracruz, Davis went to Mexico City to try to "do something" about the war. In the capital he sought an interview with Huerta, but the Mexican president was not to be dazzled by Davis' reputation, and he refused to see the correspondent. Twice Davis was jailed by federal authorities before he was permitted to return to Veracruz.[10]

In his dispatches, Davis tried to manufacture an inter-

[9] *Washington Post*, May 1, 1914, 1:2; May 4, 1914, 2:3-4.
[10] Richard Harding Davis, *Adventures and Letters* (New York, 1917), 366, 358; Gerald Langford, *The Richard Harding Davis Years* (New York, 1961), 286-289.

national incident of his detention, and he magnified and distorted the dangers of his trip to and from the capital. He wrote completely false accounts of Americans being persecuted and killed in Mexico City. Davis was contemptuous of the Mexicans, calling the women "squaws" and the men "spiggotty." He seemed determined to provoke more trouble between the United States and Mexico. In a letter to his family, Davis lamented: "It looks to me that *nothing* will induce Wilson to go to war." Back in Veracruz he wrote that the city was now "a picture of peace to delight our Secretary of State." The valiant American soldiers had become "an army of white wings," as the "apostles of peace" had "won a glorious victory." He did not criticize Funston; the general agreed wholeheartedly. But once the decision was made in Washington, Funston turned to the difficult task of restoring order to the city and populace of Veracruz. Soon most of the correspondents returned to the United States, leaving the field to the regular reporters who chronicled the day-by-day events of the military occupation.[11]

With the removal of Robert J. Kerr as governor of Veracruz, the administration became wholly military in character. Wilson had anticipated that the Mexican civilian authorities would continue to exercise their functions as they had before the coming of the Americans, that only the customs collections and port activities would need to come under military control. But the patriotism of the Mexicans and the threats from Mexico City to punish any civil employee who aided the invaders were sufficient to cause most to decline. Appeals to honor, cajolery, flattery, and plain threats (threats, for example, to bring in Cubans to do the work) succeeded in causing some to accept employment, but gradually Funston found it necessary to take control

[11] Davis, *Adventures,* 361; Davis, "When Is a War," 44, 50; *Mexican Herald,* May 10, 1914, 1:2.

of every area of government, from the municipal to the federal levels, from police and sanitation to the collection of taxes and the trying of criminal cases. It was military government in the fullest sense of the word.

The most immediate and pressing problem facing the American commander was that of public health and sanitation. This was one reason advanced by many in the United States for a quick push to Mexico City—to get the men out of the hot, malarial country. It was quite true that the mosquito season was just beginning as the Americans arrived. Whenever it rained, there were large pools of stagnant water to provide ample breeding spots for the dreaded anopheles mosquitoes. The Mexicans had made no effort to drain these or to kill off the larvae. Other diseases— smallpox, meningitis, gonorrhea, and syphilis—seemed almost endemic. There was a high mortality from tuberculosis, especially among the poorer classes. The most prevalent disease, ranging in severity from mild to fatal, was dysentery, owing to the constant heat, the flies, and the refuse and filth scattered throughout the city. There were few inside toilets in any area, and in the poor sections of the city none of any kind. Men, women, and children simply used a convenient wall, or a yard, or a street, or any place at all. To the army medical officers it was unthinkable that the troops could stay in Veracruz through the rainy season without a wholesale cleaning-up of the city.[12]

In the first days of May the military government put to work more than three thousand soldiers in a heroic effort to do away with the many years' accumulation of waste and filth. Every street, every yard, every plaza was swept out and the debris hauled to the public dump to be burned. Even the dumping ground had been neglected by the Mexican authorities before the coming of the Americans. Instead of burning the refuse, they had let it pile up. Daily

---

[12] Funston, "Report."

the dogs and vultures of the city disputed each load of freshly dumped garbage. Now oil was poured over the whole area and it was set afire. If the dumping ground was foul, this was understandable and to be expected. The worst affront to American sensibilities was the complete lack of sanitation in the public market. Here Veracruz bought almost every item of food consumed in the city. Major Paul A. Wolf, who was placed in charge of the Department of Public Works, reported to Funston: "It was almost unbearable for a white person to remain in the vicinity of the market."[13]

Because the new market had never been completed, the Americans found it, in many ways, to be in worse condition than the old. The unfinished parts permitted the easy and fast collection of waste substances. Freshly slaughtered meats, dripping blood, were hung on hooks or thrown carelessly onto the counters for display, and they were covered with flies up to the moment they were cut in portions, sold, and carried off, wrapped in old newspapers. The spare and worthless scraps were tossed under the table for the dogs and vultures. No Mexican thought it strange that these birds should make themselves at home in the refuse boxes of the market. Nor were the meat counters clean. The American inspectors found them to be pocked with holes and crevices, each one caked with old blood and crawling with maggots. The floors had been tiled, but now the tiles were broken and the cavities were "filled with the vilest fluid drained from the butchers' tables."[14]

The counters and stalls of the fish and poultry dealers were no better. The fish were scaled and eviscerated and the chickens slaughtered and plucked in the market, and the floor in those areas was covered with the accumulation

[13] P. A. Wolf, "History of the Department of Public Works," AGO File 2228507; *New York Times*, May 15, 1914, 2:3; *Mexican Herald*, May 17, 1914, 3:1-3.
[14] Wolf, "History."

of scales and feathers. The entrails were dropped on the floor, again for the dogs and birds. Old fruit and vegetables, too, were cast aside when no longer salable. Adding to the mess on the floors were the droppings of dogs and vultures and the manure and urine of burros—tethered to the outside wall—which the Indians had ridden in from the sandhills. Outside the market, against the walls, there were public urinals and toilet stalls, all uncared for and never cleaned. It was obvious to the Americans that a complete renovation of the market was imperative, and, more than that, that the old habits not be permitted to continue.[15]

The first great cleanup, then, was only the beginning. For a month a force of one thousand Mexican laborers was employed daily, building, digging, sweeping, repairing, carrying off trash and garbage. Each night the entire city area, including the market, was flushed out with sea water from the hoses of the fireboat. The army's Quartermaster Corps gave the city government one thousand large G.I. cans, and these were distributed to hotels and restaurants and placed in the streets. Sanitation was rigidly enforced in all places that sold or served food. Fines were levied, and finally even jail sentences, if garbage was not put in a can or the cans were left uncovered. "No one could say," observed one American, "that he did not know of the arrival of the garbage man, because this was always announced with bells that made more noise than the chimes in the cathedral in front of the plaza."[16]

A reporter for the *Mexican Herald,* while walking in the outskirts of the city, saw a *zopilote* swoop down in to the street to land in a garbage can, just uncovered as a street-cleaner emptied it into his cart. The Mexican managed to drive off the black scavenger with the lid of the can, but not before he was soundly beaten by the bird's wings and

15 Wolf, "History."
16 Jenkinson, "Veracruz," 141.

talons. In ordinary circumstances the vulture is the most cowardly of creatures, but hunger had made him bold and daring. When the reporter stopped to speak to the worker about it, the Mexican was perplexed, but philosophical: "That is because of the *Americanos*. The *teniente* is the devil of a master who makes us work night and day to clean the city, so that the unlucky birds of Veracruz go hungry. It is a disagreeable task, señor, but what can a gentleman do when the *Americanos* offer a man six dollars for a cart and two dollars for himself. Truly, it is not any of my affair if they care to throw away their money in the streets, and why should I not be the gainer?" No longer, he said, were the *zopilotes* to be seen in the square or on the rooftops, lazily sunning themselves. Now they drifted around in the sky trying to find something to eat. Thousands had left the city and had gone to other places in the interior. In truth, he shrugged, he "could not understand the *Americanos*." And he was right. When the military government cleaned up the city and kept it clean, most of the vultures departed. There was nothing to eat in Veracruz.[17]

After the market was flushed out, all necessary repairs were made by the Department of Public Works. Windows and doors were screened, the roof sealed, the walls calcimined, and a completely new floor of concrete was laid. The Americans also built a concrete sidewalk to replace the cobblestone walk which had been so difficult to keep clean. New public toilets were installed and kept in good condition. Flytraps were placed throughout the building. Those vendors who sold their goods outside the market were required to screen their stalls or tables. By means of strenuous measures, the flies in the market area (though they could never be completely eliminated) were kept at a minimum.[18]

[17] *Mexican Herald*, May 17, 1914, 3:1-3.
[18] *Mexican Herald*, May 17, 1914, 3:1-3; Wolf, "History."

While the Mexicans were enchanted that so much energy was being expended by the Americans in cleaning and repairing their market, they really could not understand it. They did not mind the flies. There had always been flies, and long after they were all dead, there would still be flies. Nor could they appreciate the reasons for the cleanliness, so that the military authorities encountered great difficulty in enforcing their regulations. It was one thing to install screens and quite another to keep them shut. The vendors were always forgetting to close the doors, or to put the refuse in the steel cans, or to clean off their tables. They put the flytraps under the tables to get them out of the way. The public health officers were forced to make frequent inspections of the market and the stalls. The offenders were first warned; then those who inveterately neglected the sanitation regulations were taken to the police court to be fined or jailed.[19]

The Department of Public Works was also charged with caring for the sewage and water disposal of the city. This was an important duty, for proper drainage was necessary to insure against malarial attacks among the soldiers and the Mexican population. The military government launched a vigorous program of malaria eradication. Pools were drained or covered with oil. In all, sixty-one miles of ditches were dug and 69,000 gallons of crude oil poured in the ponds. As a result, during the summer months of 1914, when the malaria incidence would normally have reached its peak, there were few mosquitoes to be seen in the city. The troops were given daily doses of quinine sulphate, and the Mexicans in the *barrios* closest to the American encampments were treated or hospitalized if they showed signs of paludism.[20]

Major Wolf's department also undertook to make as

[19] Funston, "Report."
[20] Funston, "Report."

many repairs as possible in public buildings and in the streets. When the lighting systems in all of the municipal buildings were found to be inadequate or dangerously installed, they were repaired or replaced and put in good condition. Roads were built and streets paved; an all-weather road was installed to the public dump outside the city. New bridges were erected, others repaired. The Americans constructed a large office building for the use of the military government.[21]

The supply of potable water had been completely inadequate for the city's population even before the arrival of the Americans. Now with the troops and the many other thousands of refugees crowding into Veracruz, the military government had to exercise close control over the use and the distribution of water. The problem was never entirely solved, although it was much alleviated by rationing and by strict attention to waste. Plumbing repairs, which had been avoided for years, were now made, and all water lines were kept in good condition. Ice was also in short supply, and the army experienced difficulty with the owners of the sole ice plant, who insisted on favoring their best customers, that is, the cantinas and the houses of prostitution. Funston seized the plant, and the ice was distributed through the Department of Public Works. Under American control the profits of the company more than doubled, since the owners were not required to pay bribes to the public officials of the city to stay in operation.[22]

The worst pesthole in Veracruz, though not so evident to the public eye, was the prison of San Juan de Ulúa. For several days after the port had been occupied, the Americans made no attempt to take the fortress. Incongruously, the Mexican flag was raised and lowered each day by the

---

[21] Funston, "Report."

[22] Wolf, "History"; "Sanitation in Veracruz," *Science,* n.s. XL (September 18, 1914), 406; Funston to Agwar, May 9, 1914, AGO Files, RG 94, Box 7474.

garrison of the fort, this with the gunboat *Prairie* anchored but a few yards away. After three days, however, a party of marines from *North Dakota* rowed over to the island to take charge of the fort. The Mexican commander was pleased to surrender, for there was little food left. His men had nothing to eat, he said, but black bean soup. At the order of the marine commander he threw back the great iron gates to the cell area. To the Americans it was as though a hole had suddenly been opened into Dante's Inferno. Several hundred men were huddled together in a series of cavernlike cells, each about forty feet long and fifteen feet wide. The marines were almost overcome by the stench and the maniacal outcries of the prisoners. The convicts were filthy and in rags, for each man wore the clothing he had brought with him. Many had chronic malaria and tuberculosis; nearly all had diarrhea or other enteric ailments. The condition of the political prisoners, the men who had tried to escape military service, was bad enough. But in another hole, where the criminal prisoners were incarcerated, it was even more foul. The men inside were like animals. There were no toilets in any of the cells, or in the cell area, and rats, cockroaches, spiders, and fleas infested the whole prison.

By orders of General Funston the political prisoners were given their freedom. Some returned to their homes in various parts of the Republic; others, who feared retaliation by Huerta's government, preferred to remain in Veracruz. Only those criminal prisoners who, in the judgment of the military government, had been justly convicted, were kept in custody, and these were transferred to better and more sanitary quarters in the city jail.

The cleanup of the prison was a more prodigious job than that of the market, requiring the labor of marines, sailors, and prisoners for several weeks. The walls and floors were scraped down, steamed, washed with creolin, and flushed out with firehoses. The vermin were exterminated with sulphur fumes; in all the Americans burned 1,200 pounds of sulphur. So foul were the deepest dungeons that the prisoners who worked there, performing the most noxious tasks, worked in shifts so as not to be nauseated by the odors. When the sanitary officers were finally satisfied with the condition of the prison, the cells were sealed off. The fort was used thereafter as a barracks for the marines and soldiers.[23]

The thorough housecleaning administered to Veracruz could not, however, guarantee the troops against disease or pestilence. Rigid sanitary measures were enforced in the encampments as well. All messes were screened and all food and garbage kept covered. Each soldier or marine was required to sleep under a mosquito bar. Extreme care was taken with foodstuffs in the tropical climate. Funston ordered that hashes were not to be kept overnight, nor were canned milk or canned fish to be used a second day. Green vegetables grown locally, the principal source of amoebic and bacillary dysentery, were not to be eaten raw. It was a tribute to the vigilance of the army commanders that there were only thirty-seven cases of dysentery which required hospitalization and only one death from this cause among the more than seven thousand men under the jurisdiction of the military government. Two other soldiers died in the seven-month period, one of pericarditis, the other of pneumonia "following an alcoholic debauch."[24]

The greatest single and most constant source of invalidism among the troops was venereal disease. This was to be expected, with the high incidence among the prostitutes of the

[23] Ruhl, "Unfinished Drama," 8; *Mexican Herald*, May 2, 1914, 3:5, May 12, 1914, 2:3-4, and May 28, 1914, 4:4-5; *El Dictamen*, April 30, 1914, 4:3.
[24] "Memorandum," May 27, 1914, Post Records (Veracruz), Vol. 233 (hereafter cited as PRVC); Funston, "Report"; "Report of Chief Surgeon," AGO Files, RD 6.

city, and the army and navy commanders' *laissez faire* attitude toward their men's sexual conduct. The medical officers did what they could to lessen the dangers of exposure by installing prophylactic stations in the segregated area and by rigid inspection of the prostitutes. They took advantage of the Mexican laws which required public women to register with the police. Those found to be infected were hospitalized until they were cured. Each girl received an identification card bearing her picture, her signature, and the dates she had been examined. As many as 125 women were in the hospital simultaneously with syphilis or gonorrhea.

The original segregated district was near the center of Veracruz in narrow and irregular streets. When the occupation began, the bawdy houses were found to be poorly constructed and in generally unsatisfactory condition. To make control of the traffic more efficient, the military government set aside for the enlisted men a new district on the outskirts of the city (these houses are still in use today), where the quarters were cleaner and the streets wider and more easily patrolled. No house was permitted to open until the military government had made a thorough inspection and had pronounced it sanitary. For the officers, Funston sequestered a few houses in the best residential section of Veracruz—to the great scandal of the neighbors. During the occupation there were many protests about the presence of prostitutes in this area.

The problems of the military government were compounded by the large number of foreign prostitutes who followed the troops to Veracruz. About half of these were Americans. On June 26 General Funston directed that all "public women" not of Mexican nationality would cease to "ply their trade" by July 1. Those who did not comply, he said, would be imprisoned at hard labor for six months. Any house which employed a foreign girl after that date would be closed, and any male who acted as a procurer for a non-Mexican would be confined to prison for one year at hard labor. Most of the American girls had moved to residential areas in order to cater more conveniently and discretely to the officers and American civilians. Rather than give up what had become a lucrative business, these prostitutes sent a delegation to Mexico City to protest to the Brazilian minister (who now handled American affairs in Mexico). They accused General Funston of "unwarranted restraint of trade and traffic." Their appeals were fruitless. Ever resourceful, about fifty of the foreign prostitutes then paid indigent Mexicans from five to fifty pesos to go through the civil marriage ceremony with them in order to establish their Mexican citizenship.[25]

Many decrees to enforce health and sanitation measures were published from Funston's office. There was a ban, for example, against spitting in the streets or other public places. Funston might as well have banned rain or sunshine. Much easier was the enforced vaccination of the entire population of Veracruz. Before the Americans left the city, they had vaccinated over 46,000 persons. It was not to be expected that the military government could alter the ingrained habits of the Mexicans overnight, but it did what it could by means of example, pleading, threats, and, finally, punishment. The results of the Americans' labors were demonstrated by a sharp falling off of the death rate for all diseases during the occupation. For the American troops the incidence of illness was no higher than it would have been in the United States. And for the Mexican population the death rate dropped more than 25 percent from the previous months, at a time when the rainy, hot season usually brought the highest morbidity to the city. In this

[25] "Report of Chief Surgeon"; Office of Military Governor, "Order No. 7, June 25, 1914," PVRC, Vol. 233; Funston to Agwar, June 25, 1914, Funston War Diary, 53 (hereafter cited as War Diary).

sense, the sanitation measures of the military government were an unqualified success.[26]

In legal matters the American military government hoped to confine its attention to the supervision of the occupying troops, leaving the policing of the population to the native force. This proved to be impossible, for the members of the municipal police force refused to serve the Americans for fear of subsequent punishment by the federal authorities. A completely new force was organized, directed by a Cuban who had had many years service in Mexico as a railroad detective, and who had also been chief of police in Havana during the American occupation of that island. This new corps dealt with the civilian population only. There was a large provost guard—three companies of marines and a battalion of infantry—to watch over the conduct of the American troops. The police and the courts of Veracruz were supervised by the Department of Public Safety under Major Harry A. Smith.[27]

Crimes of violence were kept at a minimum during the occupation. There were only two murders in seven months, neither involving Americans. As more and more refugees poured into the city from the interior, however, the number of robberies mounted. Many of the refugees were destitute and had no means to support themselves or their families. With the aid of the Americans the Mexican police became adept at tracking down stolen goods. Heretofore an object stolen had disappeared forever, unless one were lucky enough to encounter one's own possession in the "thieves' market." An American wrote in wonder to Major Smith: "I have lived in Mexico for eight years. I have been victimized several times, but this is the first time I have ever recovered anything." Nor was it necessary to bribe a police

[26] Jack London, "Lawgivers," *Collier's Magazine*, LIII (June 20, 1914), 15; "Report of Chief Surgeon"; "Sanitation in Veracruz," 405-406.
[27] Funston, "Report"; *El Dictamen*, May 5, 1914, 3:5.

officer to persaude him to do his duty. The law enforcement was as impartial and incorruptible as the Americans could make it. Each Sunday morning an army officer from Major Smith's department sat as a pardons court, assisted by an American woman who had been in Mexico for many years and who was interested in penal reform. Many of the lesser offenders were paroled to their employers or released outright. Concerning the dispensation of justice, Canada reported to the State Department: "It was an agreeable surprise for them, when those arrested were given their freedom."[28]

The Department of Public Safety continued the Mexican system of keeping close surveillance over the activities of the people of Veracruz. No one could give a private dance in his home, sell a banana in the streets, open a bawdy house, put up a sign, or repair a building without a permit from the police. Every morning Major Smith passed on dozens of such applications and was thus able to know what was happening in the city. The hotels and boardinghouses of Veracruz daily furnished lists of their guests and of the new arrivals in the city. It was the duty of this department, as well, to keep track of the prostitute and underworld population. When he learned that a great number of American gamblers and saloonkeepers had followed the troops to Veracruz, Major Smith ordered their summary deportation.[29]

The question of the character of the courts in Veracruz was one of the first to be considered by the occupational authorities. In a directive to General Funston, Secretary Garrison stressed that it was not to be a "belligerent" occupation, that the military government should use "leniency and liberality" in dealing with the Mexicans. "The adminis-

[28] Harry A. Smith, "Report of the Department of Public Safety," AGO File 2228507; Canada to Bryan, June 10, 1914, PRVC, Box 191.
[29] Smith, "Report."

tration of military government at Veracruz should be such as to give the inhabitants an object lesson of national good will," he wrote. As with other branches of the government of the city, the refusal of the Mexican jurists to serve under the Americans made it impossible to continue any kind of constitutional court procedure. It was decided, therefore, to establish army provost courts to deal with criminal cases. A superior provost court handled trials involving major crimes, while an inferior court took care of the lesser cases. The superior court was never busy during the occupation. In the two murder hearings, a Mexican was acquitted of slaying a fellow national and a Spaniard was convicted of slaying his mistress and sentenced to ten years in prison. There was one instance of attempted murder, robbery, and attempted rape, one of sodomy, one of burglary, and one of attempted rape. The inferior court, on the other hand, heard hundreds of cases, handing down decisions involving short jail terms or fines. Both courts sought, wherever possible, to follow the laws of Mexico in deciding the cases.

Because Mexican lawyers in Veracruz were of the opinion that the decisions of the military courts would not be binding after the occupation ceased, the Americans installed no courts to deal with civil cases. Mexicans have been accustomed, however, to conduct much of their ordinary business through courts, so that the legal department of the provost marshal's office was soon flooded with requests for the immediate adjustment of disputes at law. In each instance the department advised the litigants to settle the matter themselves, so that, without so intending, the department began to function as an equitable or arbitral court. In cases which could have been initiated before the American occupation, the officers refused to intervene, and the parties to such disputes were told to wait until the return of the Mexican authorities. If a case required immediate settlement, it was adjudicated, when possible, "under the letter and spirit" of Mexican law. If no applicable precedent or law could be found, the case was settled as commonsense and justice seemed to dictate. There was much difficulty because of the strange legal system, the foreign language problems, and the contentious habits of the Mexicans. But the fact that the courts were martial in character speeded the hearings. By the end of the occupation the legal department had a working knowledge of the Mexican civil code and the code of civil procedure, as well as the criminal code and the code of criminal procedure. The American judges felt competent to pass upon almost any question that could have been adjudicated by the Mexican courts.[30]

The thorniest problem dealt with by the legal department was that of rent disputes. During the period of anarchy which accompanied the revolutions against Díaz and Madero, and now against Huerta, many of the Mexican tenants had deferred paying their rents as long as possible, and they were now months or even years in arrears. Nearly six thousand cases involving nonpayment of rent were brought before the informal American courts. Major Smith wrote to Funston about the decisions in these cases: "Administrators of estates, collectors of rent, and owners of property have all stated that the rent questions were fairly adjudicated and expeditiously settled by this department and in a manner not at all complimentary to the previous courts."[31]

These informal courts kept no records, for the returning authorities, in any event, would not have recognized their decisions. In most of the hearings the money was paid and receipts given; thus the matter was closed. In those cases which involved mortgages, deeds of trust, or other written

[30] Garrison to Funston, May 14, 1914, AGO Files, RD 6; Funston, "Report"; Smith, "Report of the Legal Department of the Provost Marshal General's Office," AGO File 2228507.
[31] Smith, "Report of the Legal Department."

instruments, a memorandum covering the essential points of the agreement was signed by the contesting parties, and this memorandum was then taken to a notary. There the document was made legal when signed and stamped. For the Mexicans it was a most unusual experience to have legal matters settled swiftly, equitably, and, above all, at little cost to themselves. They were accustomed to proceedings which dragged on interminably and were then settled only when the judge was bribed. Whatever the Mexicans thought of the military occupation, they did not complain of the courts. The justice rendered by the Americans was incorruptible. With some degree of self-satisfaction, Major Smith described his administration: "Justice without partiality or favor has been accorded to all."[32]

At no time did Huerta recognize the right of the Americans to set up courts, either civil or criminal, in Veracruz. In the first week of June, after the mediation attempts at Niagara Falls had failed and it was apparent that the occupation would not soon end, the federal government ordered the two judges who had sat in Veracruz to move their tribunals to Soledad, the nearest large town. These courts would have jurisdiction over all criminal and civil cases originating in the canton of Veracruz. But there were many disadvantages to having a case tried in Soledad. Most of the legal records for Veracruz remained there, and there was no agreement between the American military government and the Mexican authorities on handling the records or the cases. Also, it was too expensive for the people of Veracruz to carry their litigation to Soledad. They were more than satisfied with the decisions of the Americans. The result was that the courts in Soledad had little business.[33]

The troops in Veracruz were, of course, subject to mili-

[32] Smith, "Report of the Legal Department."
[33] *Mexican Herald*, June 16, 1914, 4:4-5; *Periódico Oficial de Veracruz*, June 18, 1914, 1-2.

tary law, and about half of them were obliged to face a court martial before the end of the occupation. For the more than seven thousand men garrisoned in the city, 3,692 courts martial were convened. All but 83 of the soldiers and marines involved were convicted of the charges brought against them. The bald figures are misleading, however, for the general deportment of the troops was good, if not exemplary. There may have been instances of crimes against the Mexicans, but only one such charge of rape appears in any extant record. There were no cases of desertion and only 53 cases which culminated in a dishonorable discharge. There were no capital crimes. More than 2,400 of the charges were of a minor nature, involving unauthorized absence or drunkenness. Many of these would have brought no more than company punishment had the troops been in the United States. The frequency of this kind of delinquency was understandable, given the difficult conditions under which the men lived at Veracruz. It was hot and humid, and they had only heavy woolen clothing, so that they were uncomfortable at all times. Worst of all was the boredom. Their life was circumscribed by the perimeter around the city. They marched, they polished, they stood guard. And when they were off duty, there was the segregated district or the cantinas. If a man did not return to his encampment by "First Call," there was usually a court martial, for in a foreign country such breaches of discipline could not be tolerated.[34]

The military government was obliged early in the occupation to take charge of the postal and educational systems of Veracruz. A Department of Education was established under Major Charles Miller, with the assistance of an American civilian, F. A. De Verts. On July 22 De Verts assumed the direction of the department and controlled

[34] Blanton Winship, "Judge Advocate's Report," AGO File 2228507; Funston, "Report."

the schools and the library until the evacuation of the troops. It required much tact and persuasion and a great deal of hard work on the part of the Americans to reorganize the public school system. All of the schools had been closed on the day of the initial landing, and it was not until May 12 that any were reopened. By the end of the month all were functioning again, although a few former officials urged the parents to send their children to private schools rather than to those maintained by the "invaders." Many of the teachers were reluctant to work under the Americans, but Major Miller appealed to their sense of duty to the children (and even at one time threatened to bring in teachers from Cuba), and most did return eventually to their classrooms. On June 8 the department organized a teachers' institute, the first of its kind in Veracruz, which was received with enthusiasm. During July and August the schools were closed for their regular vacations, but in the fall all opened again with greater attendance than ever before. The school system was functioning well when the Americans left in November.[35]

Until May 3 the post office of Veracruz was under the direction of Commander J. M. Luby of *South Carolina,* who had supervised the initial cleaning-up in the building. On that date he was relieved by an American civilian, H. M. Robinson, a member of the United States postal service, who had been sent from Galveston at the request of General Funston. When Robinson took control of the mail system, he found that Commander Luby had been sending mailbags destined for the interior to the gap in the rail lines beyond the American perimeter. After a week the military government discovered that the troops of General Maass had made no attempt to receive the mail, and that more than two hundred sacks were still lying beside the tracks. All deliveries were then halted until May 25, when an

[35] Funston, "Report."

agreement was reached between the governments of the United States and Mexico for the mutual exchange of mail.

From the beginning Robinson tried to give the Mexicans "as good or better service than they were accustomed to before." All mail to the exterior or within Veracruz was required to bear American postage, but letters to the rest of Mexico could be sent with either Mexican or American stamps. The postal department soon found, however, that the Mexican government was requiring the recipients of mail from Veracruz to pay for delivery, unless the letters or parcels bore Mexican postage. In order to avoid double payment, most people in Veracruz then used Mexican stamps.

The post office was put in good condition by the military government. It was thoroughly cleaned, all broken windows replaced, and new padlocks installed on all of the doors. For the most part the operations of the postal system were self-sustaining. Good service was given at a lower cost than before the occupation.[36]

It was the intent of the American government that the full cost of the occupation—except for the military expenditures—should be borne by the people of Veracruz. The military government must pay for itself from the regular revenues collected in Veracruz before the seizure of the city. For this purpose Funston created a Department of Finance under Captain Harold B. Fiske. It was a difficult job, for Captain Fiske had to collect municipal, state, and federal taxes, account for them all, and disburse them separately. His office combined the functions of what had hitherto been three separate taxing agencies. As General Funston observed in a report to the War Department: "To collect taxes was no slight task, when Mexican practices are taken into consideration." Federal revenues, aside from the import and export duties, came almost exclusively from

---

[36] Funston to Agwar, May 11, 1914, AGO Files, RG 94, Box 7480; H. M. Robinson, "Report," November 29, 1914, AGO File 2228507.

the sale of stamps required by law to be placed on all documents and records. In addition, the government of Huerta had decreed a stamp tax of 30 percent on all state and municipal levies. These were collected in Veracruz by Fiske's department and held in a separate account to be turned over to the federal government at the end of the occupation. The import and export duties came under the jurisdiction of the administrator of customs and were collected and accounted for separately. The state revenues were derived mostly from taxes on commercial and industrial establishments, real estate, slaughterhouses, peddlers, annuities, leases, and inheritances. These monies, too, were held for payment later to the state government of Verucruz-Llave.[37]

The military government was confronted immediately with the problem of obtaining revenues for the municipal administration in the face of mounting costs and decreasing sources of funds. When the city government was taken over, only 30,000 pesos were found in the treasury, and this small sum vanished quickly to help pay for the great cleanup of the port. Ordinarily, municipal revenues came from licenses and charges for stall and floorspace in the public market, peddlers, slaughtering fees, water, entertainment permits, gambling concessions, and the bullfights. Although the Wilson administration obtained an additional appropriation from Congress to finance the sanitation measures, and the army provided the garbage cans and the materials for screening the markets, it was soon apparent that the city offices must practice the strictest of economies. Since the city was now shut off from the rest of the country, there was a heavy slump in business and in the tourist trade, with a consequent loss of municipal revenues. A major blow to a balanced budget was an order from the military governor which canceled the gambling concessions (these alone had

[37] Funston, "Report."

brought the city 13,000 pesos a month) and banned bullfights in Veracruz. The establishment of military tribunals
cost the city its income from court fees. And the financial
situation was made even worse by an inflation of the peso
at the time that the revenues were falling off.

Yet in spite of the extraordinary expenditures and the
cost of training new and inefficient employees in almost
every municipal office, the city government under the
Americans remained solvent. Formerly, there had been a
heavy leakage of public funds into the pockets of city officials. Now corruption was ended. The administration of
Veracruz was completely honest. This alone would have
balanced the budget in ordinary times. Then the military
governor learned that under Mexican law the city might
borrow money from the state of Veracruz-Llave. By the
expedient of shifting funds from one account to another,
the Department of Finance obtained sufficient revenue to
guarantee the municipal budget. Although this left the city
government in debt to the state when the American occupation ended, Funston estimated that a month's return
from the gambling concessions, the bullring, and lottery
tickets would wipe out this indebtedness.[38]

With the unsettled conditions throughout Mexico and
the lack of communication between the occupation authorities and the federal government in Mexico City, there was
a chronic and almost insoluble problem of currency in
Veracruz. From the first there was a shortage of bills of
denominations smaller than five pesos. The Mexicans
hoarded the gold and silver coins and would not put them
into circulation. At the same time, there was no confidence
in the late issue currency of Huerta, for the Constitutionalists
had made it plain that they would not assume responsibility for any financial acts of Huerta's regime. This dearth

[38] H. B. Fiske (?), "Report of Department of Finance," AGO File
2228507; Funston, "Report."

of small currency made difficult the conduct of business in the city. Some of the larger business houses paid a premium for fractional currency, and from time to time the banks of Veracruz were able to smuggle bills through the federal lines. The situation was improved in July when the Chamber of Commerce issued a scrip in denominations of 10, 25, and 50 centavos, secured by a deposit of 20,000 pesos in one of the city's large banks. It would be redeemed in 5-peso lots within three years. Although there was no attempt at the forced circulation of this scrip, it gained public confidence, since it could be used in paying taxes. A new problem appeared with the overthrow of Huerta in July and the institution of a revolutionary regime in Mexico City. The new currency printed by the Constitutionalists soon made its appearance in Veracruz, but the military government refused to accept any but prerevolutionary bills in taxes and in payment for customs charges. The problem had not been resolved when the occupation was ended and Veracruz was taken over by the Carrancistas.[39]

Although the military government ultimately took over almost all of the functions of the previous civil regime, the control of the customs service was its most important duty and the reason for the presence of the armed forces in Veracruz. Early in the afternoon of April 21, after firing had broken out in the city, bluejackets from *Utah* entered the customhouse and warehouses to find that the offices had been ransacked by the Mexicans. Desks were pried open, and there were many damaged cases scattered about. Most of the customs officials and guards had fled, though a few were found hiding in the buildings. These were rounded up and taken into custody. During the next day and a half, in which the customs area was under fire, the warehouses were evacuated and reoccupied many times by detachments from the various ships in the fleet. No one

[39] *Mexican Herald,* June 13, 1914, 3:4; Fiske (?), "Report."

thought or cared to guard the area against pilferage or damage. On the morning of the twenty-third, with the end of hostilities, a group of bluejackets from *San Francisco* were ordered to take charge of the area. On their arrival they found American sailors and marines looting the buildings. The commanding officer, Lieutenant W. J. Giles, drove the American vandals out, but he made no arrests and did not report the looting to Admiral Fletcher. By now the buildings were in complete disorder. Boxes were smashed open and their contents thrown onto the floor. Every desk and locker in the customhouse and the warehouses was broken into and rifled. Though there had been some damage before the Americans came, most of it was caused by their own lack of discipline and their personal dishonesty.[40]

One of Admiral Fletcher's first appointments after the occupation was that of Commander Herman O. Stickney as administrator of customs for the port, a position he continued to hold under the military government of General Funston. On taking charge, Stickney conferred with Mariano Azcarraga, the Mexican customs collector, to ask him to continue in his office under the Americans. But Azcarraga refused, pointing out—as had the other public officials —the severe penalties he might incur. Nor would he open the safe in his office or give the Americans the combination until he was forced to do so. Stickney made a careful inventory of the contents and gave Azcarraga a receipt. Whatever business was conducted by the port would be done by the Americans alone. Even the ship pilots of Veracruz refused to guide foreign vessels into the harbor. Stickney's first job was to supervise the landing of *Ypiranga*.

For two days the German ship rode at anchor outside the harbor before, on April 23, she was given permission to come in and discharge the cargo. *Ypiranga's* captain re-

[40] H. O. Stickney, "Report on Operations of Custom Service," AGO File 2228507.

fused to land the arms, indicating to the Americans that they would be returned to Germany. Without creating another international incident, there was nothing that Stickney could do to force him to release his cargo. Besides, taking the arms back to Hamburg would serve the same purpose, so long as Huerta did not receive the shipment. On April 29, Secretary of State Bryan formally thanked the German imperial government for its decision to recall the shipment. Seemingly the issue had been resolved.[41]

But the *Ypiranga* affair did not end here. The ship remained in Veracruz for several days, picking up cargo and refugees who wished to leave Mexico, before sailing on May 3 to Tampico and, ultimately, Mobile, Alabama. Despite the assurances of *Ypiranga's* captain, the vessel did not proceed to Europe. Instead, after taking more passengers and goods aboard, the ship returned to Mexican waters. On May 27, *Ypiranga* put into Puerto México, south of Veracruz, to discharge her cargo of arms. After a long and circuitous voyage, much international tension, and armed conflict, the weapons and ammunition reached their destination. They were delivered intact in Mexico City. In a sense, Wilson had been foiled by the maneuvering of the German captain. Yet by now, with the American forces in control of Veracruz, the president had lost interest in the shipment. Robert Lansing, speaking for Woodrow Wilson, told the press: "We have nothing to do with what is landed [at Puerto México]."[42]

And there was yet another chapter to the story of *Ypiranga*. When the ship returned to Veracruz, after dropping her cargo at Puerto México, Stickney refused to furnish clearing papers on the ground that the goods had been consigned to Veracruz. Under Mexican law he could fine

[41] Stickney, "Report"; Bryan to J. H. Bernstorff, April 29, 1914 /11922a.
[42] *Mexican Herald*, May 3, 1914, 3:3-4; *New York World*, May 28, 1914, 1:6; Funston to Agwar, May 27, 1914, War Diary, 37.

a ship's master for this evasion of consignment. On May 30, Stickney levied a penalty of nearly 900,000 pesos against the Hamburg-American Line. Although the captain refused to pay the assessment, the ship was finally permitted to sail when the company's agents in Veracruz gave bond in the amount of the fine. Stickney was legally correct in imposing the fine, but Wilson and the State Department did not wish to offend the German government. Secretary of War Garrison ordered Funston to cancel the assessment, and the incident was closed. As for the shipment of arms, it came too late to save Huerta.[43]

The customs station had been one of the most graft-ridden agencies in Veracruz before the American occupation. As in any port, there were many opportunities for bribery and especially for petty thievery. Now no one could escape paying duties—as some had done earlier—through bribery of the inspectors or through favoritism; and after Stickney took control of the office, there was only one major theft. On the night of May 27, valuable jewels disappeared from a passenger's baggage, although the luggage was open to view from all sides and Mexican officials and American soldiers guarded it. No trace of the jewels was ever found. In spite of the fact that most of the employees who were persuaded to work for Stickney had had no experience in their positions, and they were not required to obtain bonds, there were fewer thefts than before the occupation. The port officials continued to strive for absolute honesty, but the number and the frequency of directives was ample proof that venality and peculation were difficult, at best, to control. Stevedores were not permitted to wear *chamarras,* loose-fitting blouses with large pockets which facilitated pilferage. All employees were forbidden to allow outsiders to sweep up or to remove waste around opened merchandise,

[43] Funston to Agwar, May 30, 1914, War Diary, 41; Garrison to Funston, June 5, 1914, War Diary, 44.

and the Mexican customs inspectors could no longer take "samples" from the goods they were required to inspect. Although Commander Stickney could never eliminate all of the troubles which beset his office, he was able to improve the service in the customhouse, while at the same time cutting the costs. The checking of baggage and of merchandise was speeded up and made more efficient, and dishonesty was kept at a minimum.[44]

The job of collecting import and export duties was complicated by the currency problems in Veracruz. A year earlier, Huerta's government had decreed that all duties would be paid in certificates, which could be purchased only in silver, issued through the Banco Nacional. This method of payment was to insure the setting aside of the receipts from customs for the service on certain bond issues, principally French, which formed part of the national debt of Mexico. Since silver was required to obtain the certificates, the duties were, in effect, to be paid in specie. This decree was later modified so that payment could also be made in the notes of certain Mexican banks. Then in early April, just before the crisis with the United States, the order to make payments in silver certificates was reinstated. The question of the mode of payment was thus confused when the Americans seized the port, for some banknotes were still being accepted at the customhouse. Under Stickney's administration the collectors did not insist on payment in silver certificates, for none could be obtained in Veracruz. Consequently, Huerta's government demanded that goods brought into the interior pay another duty in silver. Although the American State Department remonstrated with Huerta and tried to persuade him to halt the imposition of double duties, no satisfactory solution was found. And after the Constitutionalists replaced Huerta in Mexico City,

[44] Stickney, "Report"; Funston, "Report"; E. L. Beach, "Circular," July 24, 1914, AGO File 2228507.

the second payment was still required. Neither Huerta nor Carranza would concede to the American military government the right to collect duties.[45]

From time to time Constitutionalist currency was offered in payment of duties, but it was not accepted by Stickney, even though Carranza had voided the notes issued by Huerta's government. When the occupation ceased in November, the military government had accumulated a large amount of currency in Veracruz, but there was no one to give it to. The regime of Carranza insisted that these notes were no longer legal tender. As the Americans evacuated the city, they carried with them strongboxes filled with the Huertista bills. No decision on their disposition could be made until Mexico had found a constitutional government.[46]

Under the military regime the Mexicans in Veracruz had no voice in running their own government. The city council did not meet. Not a single important public servant remained in office. This was all of their own doing, the consequence of their refusal to aid the invaders in any way. In effect, the American government was a despotism for the seven months the troops occupied the city. Yet it was by all counts a benevolent despotism, the best government the people of Veracruz had ever had. Though the first concern of the American commanders was always the well-being of their own men, as a result of their labors, Veracruz was the cleanest, most efficient, most honestly and justly governed city in all of Mexican history. The American forces had no right to be in Mexico. They had killed hundreds of Mexicans to take the city. But there is no denying that much good accompanied the invasion. Babies lived who might otherwise have died of disease. Buildings and streets were left in a good state of repair. Municipal finances were sound. However the Mexicans felt—and have since felt—

---

[45] "Report of Fiscal Officer" (no date), AGO File 2228507.
[46] Funston to Agwar, August 5, 1914, AGO Files, RG 94, Box 7480.

about the occupation, the record of the military government was in the highest tradition of American service to
mankind. Setting aside the high initial cost of the landing,
Woodrow Wilson could be proud of the accomplishments
of the men he had sent to Mexico.

FIVE

The Evacuation

FRANCISCO VILLA and Venustiano Carranza did not trust each other from the moment of their initial meeting in 1914. Said Villa later: "I embraced him energetically, but with the first few words we spoke my blood turned to ice. I saw that I could not open my heart to him. As far as he was concerned, I was a rival, not a friend. He never looked me in the eye and during our entire conversation emphasized our differences in origin, pointing out to me that he had been everything from municipal president, *jefe políticc,* governor, and senator to First Chief. And he lectured me on things like decrees and laws which I could not understand. . . . There was nothing in common between that man and me."[1]

These two men represented the ultimate poles of the Constitutionalist revolution. Carranza was middle-class respectability, dull, uninspiring, and long-winded in speech. Though he commanded respect, he was too detached from his fellow men to be either loved or hated. He drew political inspiration from the great politicians of the nineteenth century: Benito Juárez, Melchor Ocampo, Miguel and Sebastián Lerdo. His aim as first chief of the Constitutionalist forces was to turn Mexico's political clock back to those pre-Porfirian halcyon days of Liberalism. He rejected social and economic reforms, unless they should come gradually and legally within the constitution. Throughout his revolutionary career, Carranza insisted stubbornly that Mexico's government must be civilian, that militarism and pretorianism were endemic evils to be extirpated upon the success of his revolution. By his stubbornness, he precipitated the break with General Villa which threw his country into a bloody and protracted civil war.

Villa, in contrast, was all that Carranza was not: virile, earthy, passionate, given to emotional outbursts. He could ruthlessly threaten death in one moment and embrace his intended victim with protestations of affection and esteem in the next. He inspired love and loyalty, fear and loathing. Villa was peon Mexico, as Carranza was her educated city-dwelling middle class. Because he sprang from the soil, he loved the peasants of the countryside. The revolution, so far as he was concerned, would bring land to the landless, more food, better housing, and, perhaps, more education. And these reforms would be brought about in the present and by direct action, not through any long-drawn-out legal process. Estates would be seized, enemies of the people eliminated. The revolution could be either Carranza's or Villa's. It could not be both.

So long as Villa and Carranza had in Victoriano Huerta a common enemy, their rivalry was kept within reasonable bounds. But on July 15, 1914, Huerta resigned his claim to the presidency of Mexico and went into exile. Although the first chief occupied Mexico City and assumed control of the national government, Villa refused to recognize Carranza as his superior. Mexico moved inexorably toward a new

[1] Ramón Puente, *Vida de Francisco Villa contada por el mismo* (Los Angeles, 1919), 78.

war, as the victorious revolution fell upon itself and devoured its own vitals.

To Woodrow Wilson, Huerta's downfall came as welcome news, for his policies—following, it is true, a long and a tortuous path—seemed finally to have borne good fruit. Soon, it was expected, Carranza would convoke new elections, and a democratic government, genuinely representative of the Mexican people, would take shape. Yet Carranza delayed, preferring to continue the informal, extralegal, preconstitutional regime of the first chieftaincy. The congress did not meet; there were no courts, no judges. Carranza issued decrees as they were needed, and Mexico's government remained revolutionary. In this way, Carranza thought, he might deal more effectively with the ex-Huertistas, who were now to be held responsible for the crimes, real or fanciful, of the Huerta administration. Moreover, there could be no genuine national government until both Zapata and Villa were brought to heel. This was the aim of Carranza as he summoned a "junta of chiefs" to meet in Mexico City on October 1.[2]

By the end of August it was apparent, to Woodrow Wilson's great disappointment, that Carranza had no intention of holding elections. Undeterred by the failure of earlier amateur diplomats in Mexico, the president sent another special agent, Paul Fuller, to try to wring from the first chief promises for the restoration of constitutional government. Fuller got nowhere with Carranza. In the first place, he was a Catholic, and the revolutionaries suspected his motives. And secondly, Carranza held that the question of elections was not one for international discussion, that it must be decided by the Mexicans alone. When Fuller met the first chief in Mexico City during the first week of September, Carranza refused to hear any word about elections. The "junta of chiefs" would determine when these would

[2] Quirk, *Mexican Revolution*, 68.

be held, he told Fuller. Carranza was interested only in the evacuation of Veracruz.[3]

For Carranza it was of the utmost importance that he secure control of that port. His administration could not continue to print paper currency with no other backing than the force of the Constitutionalist armies. Because so much of the revenue of the federal government came from the import and export duties, it was imperative that he have Veracruz before hostilities broke out with Villa's Division of the North. Also, if war did come, Carranza would need the port to supply his armies. The American government, too, could not postpone a decision on Veracruz. The city had been seized as an act of retaliation against Huerta, who was now out of office, and Wilson could no longer maintain that the possession of Veracruz was directed against a man and his policies, and not against the Mexican people. From the outside, the rent in the body of the revolution did not seem irremediable; the report that Carranza intended to call an assembly of revolutionary leaders to discuss elections assured Wilson that peace would soon be restored. He instructed the State Department to begin negotiations with Carranza on the evacuation of the American troops.

On September 16—Mexico's Independence Day—John R. Silliman, the American vice consul in Veracruz, and Cardoso de Oliveira went to the National Palace to tell Carranza that the troops would be withdrawn. They asked the first chief to designate some "responsible authority" to whom the customhouse and the other offices of the city could be delivered. In reply, Carranza said that General Cándido Aguilar, Constitutionalist governor of the state of Veracruz, would take charge of the port facilities. On the basis of this oral agreement it seemed that within a few days the soldiers and marines would be embarked and that the

3 Silliman to Bryan, September 8, 1914 /13133.

military occupation of the city would cease. The army ordered a number of transports to proceed to Veracruz to pick up the men and their equipment.[4]

What had seemed so simple to Washington and to Mexico City presented problems, nevertheless, in the city of Veracruz. General Funston told Garrison that he needed at least four weeks to assure an orderly transfer of authority to the Constitutionalists. The Americans had labored mightily and conscientiously to give Veracruz the best possible government, and they did not wish to see their accomplishments destroyed by a hasty and thoughtless action. To leave without adequate preparation would only precipitate anarchy in the administration of the city. He asked that Carranza send his officials to Veracruz so that they could work alongside the Americans for sufficient time to be adequately trained when the evacuation came. But more important than this problem, said Funston, were the threats against those in Veracruz who had served the Americans and against the refugees who had fled from the interior to escape the revolutionaries. Constitutionalist agents were circulating in the city, he said, making a list of those marked for punishment. When the news of the impending departure of the Americans was published, hundreds of Mexicans crowded the offices of the steamship lines, seeking some means of leaving the country before the arrival of the Constitutionalists. In addition, said Funston, Carranza's agents had announced that all those merchants who had paid import duties to the American military government on goods brought into Mexico would be required to pay again to the Constitutionalist regime. Funston asked Washington to secure guarantees from Carranza, before the evac-

[4] Bryan to Cardoso de Oliveira, September 15, 1914, Post Records (Mexico City), 1914/800 (hereafter cited as PRMC); Silliman to Bryan, September 16, 1914 /13196; Garrison to Funston, September 15, 1914, War Diary, 84; Cardoso de Oliveira to Bryan, September 17, 1914, PRMC 1914/800.

uation, that there would be no attacks on those who had worked for the Americans or on the refugees, and that no double duties would be levied.[5]

Neither Carranza nor Aguilar showed any interest in effecting an orderly transfer of the port. Despite General Funston's offer to work with the Mexican officials, none arrived in Veracruz. Instead, Aguilar sent a colonel from his staff to request that the Americans turn over all of their outposts immediately, including the water station at El Tejar. The Constitutionalists were concerned only with revenging themselves upon the fifteen thousand hapless refugees. Aguilar told Funston he wanted to throw a tight cordon of troops around the city so that none could escape.[6]

President Wilson did not learn of Funston's message until the morning of September 21, when he conferred with Garrison about the planned evacuation. The possibility that there might be another charge against those who had paid duties or fees to the American customs agents in good faith and that the Mexicans who had worked for the military government would be punished by the Constitutionalists for their collaboration offended the president's sense of what was right and proper. Wilson directed Robert Lansing, the acting secretary of state, to advise Carranza that the occupation could not be terminated until the Constitutionalist government guaranteed that there would be no punitive measures of this nature.[7]

Wilson was less interested in the fate of the refugees. Since they had fled the revolutionaries, they must have been tarred with the brush of the murderer and usurper Victoriano Huerta. If they were guilty, they should be pun-

[5] Funston to Agwar, September 17, 1914 /13251; Funston to Agwar, September 17, 1914, War Diary, 86-89; Agwar to Funston, September 18, 1914, War Diary, 88.

[6] Funston to Agwar, September 21, 1914, War Diary, 90.

[7] Garrison to Bryan, September 21, 1914 /11384; Lansing to Cardoso de Oliveira, September 22, 1914, PRMC 1914/800.

ished. As a result of his conference with the president, Garrison told Funston to give public notice in Veracruz that the American government could not assume any responsibility for the safety of Mexican citizens, even those who had been employed by the military regime, and that no transportation could be furnished to the United States. Unless the refugees could secure passage on one of the regular private liners, they must take their chances when the city changed hands. This announcement, made by Funston with all reluctance, virtually paralyzed the city government, for most of the Mexican employees began to make plans to leave. They had been led to believe, when they had accepted positions with the Americans, that they would be protected. Now it seemed that they were being thrown to the wolves. Morale disintegrated, and no one cared to perform the duties of his office. In the customs service, directives came daily from Commander Stickney's office as he sought to restore order. The clerks, he said, were "wandering away from work," talking loudly "on subjects foreign to customs house business," playing, or engaging in "improper conduct." He ordered that these practices cease under the penalty of heavy fines. Whatever directives Stickney or others in the military government might give, however, all of the Mexicans knew that soon the Constitutionalists would be in Veracruz and that they were defenseless.[8]

With the arrival of the army transports in Veracruz, the troops began to pack their equipment for storage aboard the ships. Only a field allowance for each contingent, sufficient to clothe and house the men, was left ashore. When the ships were loaded, they were moved beyond the break-

[8] Garrison to Funston, September 22, 1914, War Diary, 91; Funston to Agwar, September 23, 1914, AGO Files, RG 94, Box 7478; Garrison to Funston, September 24, 1914, AGO Files, RG 94, Box 7478; Stickney, "Order," October 16, 1914, AGO File 2228507.

waters to anchor in the outer harbor, so that commercial vessels might use the docking facilities of the port. In uneasy suspense the troops and the citizens of Veracruz waited for the final order of withdrawal. As days lengthened into weeks without an evacuation, equipment or food had to be unpacked and removed from the ships' holds, and taken ashore. Funston was forced to keep the ships at anchor, ready to sail at a moment's notice, so as to comply with any possible order from Washington.[9]

By the end of the month the State Department had received no reply from Carranza concerning the guarantees. In defiance of the demands of Woodrow Wilson, the first chief was as determined to maintain Mexican sovereignty and honor as was Victoriano Huerta before him. This was not a question, he believed, to be settled between his government and the United States. On October 1, Bryan asked Cardoso de Oliveira to bring the matter again to the attention of the Mexican government. Now that the decision had been made to withdraw from Veracruz, Wilson was anxious to pull the troops out as soon as possible. He told Bryan that for the United States "to linger longer in our departure . . . would make a very bad impression not only in Mexico, but in Latin America generally." He hoped "that the Department's correspondence with the temporary authorities in Mexico City has resulted in something definite which we can use as a basis for handing over the civil authority on our departure." When Carranza finally answered the American message on October 5, he made no reference to the guarantees. Cándido Aguilar had already been given "full instructions," the first chief said, to receive the port from the Americans.[10]

9 Funston, "Report."
10 Bryan to Cardoso de Oliveira, October 1, 1914, PRMC 1914/800; Wilson to Bryan, October 2, 1914 /13407; Cardoso de Oliveira to Bryan, October 5, 1914, PRMC 1914/800.

Annoyed by Carranza's failure to give an adequate reply, Wilson asked the State Department to deliver another and firmer note, demanding a "clear, explicit, and public" statement as the price for American withdrawal. Carranza must guarantee, said Wilson, that "no new duties would be collected" and that no punishment would be inflicted upon the population, "except those guilty of crimes," with the understanding that the acceptance of employment under the American authorities was not to be construed as "criminal or otherwise prejudicial."[11]

Another week passed before Carranza answered this new note, and again his reply was noncommittal. He was referring the matter, he said, to the Convention at Aguascalientes for its decision. On October 17 the members of the Convention met in secret session and voted to instruct Carranza to concede the required decrees. But Carranza was only procrastinating in the hope of wearing down the resistance of Woodrow Wilson. He had no intention of publishing the decrees, whatever the Convention might recommend. Five days later, he gave his final answer to the State Department. He said he "could not make any statement or issue any manifesto to comply with the requests of the American government, as the affairs to which such requests have reference ought to be of the exclusive initiative of the Mexican authorities." In conclusion, he asked the Americans to proceed in naming a date for the evacuation.[12]

By the end of October the issue had not been settled. Neither Carranza nor Wilson would concede an inch to the other. Isidro Fabela, who handled foreign affairs in the

[11] Bryan to Cardoso de Oliveira, October 7, 1914, PRMC 1914/800.

[12] J. W. Belt to Bryan, October 12, 1914 /13476; Cardoso de Oliveira to Bryan, October 14, 1914, PRMC 1914/800; Z. L. Cobb (for Leon J. Canova) to Bryan, October 18, 1914 /13528; Silliman to Bryan, October 19, 1914 /13537; Cardoso de Oliveira to Bryan, October 22, 1914, PRMC 1914/800.

unofficial cabinet of the first chief, told American representatives privately that no one would be molested in Veracruz who had served the military government and that no back duties or taxes would be collected. It would be "inexpedient," he confided, for Carranza to make a public declaration to that effect, as Wilson demanded. In Washington and in Mexico City, national pride and personal intransigence made each side willing to wait for the retreat of the other. In Veracruz, the situation was fast becoming critical.[13]

For a month and a half the American troops had been living in the daily expectation that they would soon return to the United States, and now many of the men required new clothing or equipment. Three of the army regiments were quartered in tents. While these tents had provided adequate housing during the warm weather, in November the season of the northers would set in, bringing cold rains and violent storms. Funston cabled the War Department on October 30 asking for a quick decision as to whether his men would stay or leave. If they were staying, he said, they would need more permanent quarters, for the residents of Veracruz were of the "unanimous opinion" that army tents were too flimsy to withstand the force of a norther. There had been "three mild ones" so far, in which the winds had reached "only sixty miles per hour," and these had torn many of the tents to shreds, Funston said. If better housing was to be erected, he would need to import lumber from the United States.[14]

It was clear that a solution to the diplomatic stalemate could not long be delayed. In the end it was Carranza who backed down, not because he was less stubborn than the American president or because he was converted by Wilson's logic, but because a worsening of the split in the

13 Silliman to Bryan, October 22, 1914 /13570.
14 Funston to Agwar, October 30, 1914, AGO Files, RG 94, Box 7478.

ranks of the revolutionaries caused him to flee Mexico City. Within a few days he was to need Veracruz badly as a haven of refuge from his enemies.

When Carranza's "junta of chiefs" met in Mexico City on October 1, the majority of the delegates had already agreed to move to Aguascalientes. Carranza had intended that the body have no permanence, that its functions would be purely consultative. He firmly believed in civilian precedence in the government, and he would not concede that a group of revolutionaries with no legal standing could make decisions affecting the political destinies of the Mexican people. Most of the representatives, however, were military men who disdained the civilian as a slacker who would not take up arms to defend his principles, as they had done. Whatever Carranza might think, the course of the revolution was in the hands of the soldiers. Led by Alvaro Obregón, the delegates called themselves a Convention, not a "junta," and voted to move their sessions to Aguascalientes as a gesture of reconciliation to the Villistas, who had not been invited to Mexico City. And as a final act of independence from the first chief, the civilians were to be excluded from any participation in the affairs of the Convention.[15]

In Aguascalientes, the military delegates, reinforced by the representatives from Villa and Zapata, moved quickly to heal the breach in the revolution. They voted the "resignation" of Carranza and his replacement with another general satisfactory to all factions. The choice fell on Eulalio Gutiérrez, who had done so little in the revolution that he had incurred no man's enmity. Carranza's reaction was immediate and vehement. He withdrew his own delegates and prepared for war with the seditious members of the Convention. No one, not even Obregón, could prevent hostilities, for the quarrel between Villa and Carranza was too

---

[15] Quirk, *Mexican Revolution*, 87-100.

bitter to be settled by words of peace. In the end, Obregón sided with Carranza. He had been willing to jettison the first chief, if this could save the revolution. But Villa and Zapata stood for lawlessness and cruelty, and Obregón could see no hope for the future of Mexico under their banners.[16]

In the early days of November, Mexico fell into two armed camps, that of the Convention, supported by Francisco Villa's Division of the North and Emiliano Zapata's Liberating Army of the South, and that of the Constitutionalists under Carranza, Obregón, and Pablo González. Great battles were to be fought, more bitter and bloody than any in Mexico's history, and ultimately Carranza, with the inspired military leadership of Obregón, would triumph. But as hostilities began, the outlook for the Constitutionalists seemed bleak. Villa and the Convention had the larger, the better equipped armies. Many of Carranza's supporters defected to Villa in the anticipation that he would win. Faced with overwhelming odds, Carranza evacuated Mexico City, falling back to Puebla and then to Córdoba in the state of Veracruz. He was ready now to yield to Wilson and to give the required guarantees. To hold Veracruz was his only hope for victory.

On November 9 the first chief issued from Córdoba a general amnesty for all Mexicans who had served the American government in Veracruz. And on the following day Isidro Fabela advised the State Department that Carranza was ready to make further concessions. A petition had been circulated in Veracruz by the Chamber of Commerce, he said, indicating that the commercial interests in the city were satisfied that they would receive fair treatment from the Constitutionalists. It was signed also, said Fabela, by the employees of the customhouse. In view of the feelings spontaneously expressed by the people of Veracruz, Ca-

16 Quirk, *Mexican Revolution*, 101-131.

rranza was willing to guarantee that no further exactions would be made in cases where duties had already been paid. Consul Canada warned his superiors that the petition, far from being spontaneous, had been prepared by a colonel in the forces of Cándido Aguilar. But Wilson was satisfied with Carranza's apparent capitulation, and he ordered the evacuation to proceed. On November 13, Bryan stated that in view of the fact that the guarantees had been given by both the Convention and Carranza, the American occupation would be terminated in ten days. There was no indication as to which faction would receive the port.[17]

The new announcement in Veracruz that the Americans were definitely leaving brought yet another wave of panic among the refugees who had not been able to secure passage to the United States. Crowds of Mexicans—many of them employees of the military government—besieged the American consulate protesting that the promises of Carranza were worthless. Stickney offered to take those employees who wished to leave on American ships, but the American government had no means of taking care of all of the refugees. With the acquiescence of the War Department, which reversed its earlier stand, Funston was able to charter a number of private vessels to evacuate many of the Mexicans.[18]

Funston's orders from the War Department made no mention of delivering the city to either of the revolutionary factions. As between the Convention and the Constitutionalists, the American government would maintain strict neutrality. Yet it was clear, even as the troops prepared to embark, who would occupy Veracruz. Though Villa announced that he would take charge of the city, and Zapata echoed

[17] *Gaceta Oficial de Veracruz*, November 17, 1914, 1-4; Cardoso de Oliveira to Bryan, November 10, 1914, PRMC 1914/800; Canada to Bryan, November 11, 1914 /13755; Bryan to Cardoso de Oliveira, November 13, 1914, PRMC 1914/800.
[18] Henry Breckinridge to Funston, November 20, 1914, War Diary, 124; Stickney, "Order," November 13, 1914, AGO File 2228507.

with threats to move in the troops of Higinio Aguilar or Benjamín Argumedo, only the Constitutionalists were close enough to take advantage of the American departure. And in this fortuitous proximity lay the ultimate salvation of the first chief. That he was able to defeat both Zapata and Villa in the long run was due to his ability to supply his armies through the port of Veracruz.[19]

The men of Funston's command were ready to go—they had been ready for nearly two months. All that was required of the military government was to put the offices in good condition, to audit the funds for the last time, and to leave the city in order. Funston would bring with him the monies collected by Stickney's office, since no decision could be made at that point as to which faction would receive the customs funds. Moreover, some of the funds had been earmarked by Huerta for the French government, and this too needed to be cleared up by negotiation with the Mexicans. By the evening of the twenty-second all was in readiness. All offices were cleaned and locked; the keys were given to the Chamber of Commerce. The books and records of the various departments were deposited with Canada in the American consulate to prove the integrity of the military administration. Mules and horses used by the mail service were watered and fed and tethered outside the post office.[20]

Early on the morning of November 23 the long-delayed evacuation began. The marines guarding the water station at El Tejar were pulled back to the city, followed closely by the entire outpost line in the sandhills surrounding Veracruz. In the city the provost guards remained alert on every street corner to prevent disturbances by the civil population. The city was quiet, however, and there was no sign of hostility against the troops. Many women wept

[19] Funston to Agwar, November 20, 1914, War Diary, 124.
[20] Funston to Agwar, November 20, 1914, AGO Files, RG 94, Box 7480; Funston to Agwar, November 21, 1914, AGO Files, RG 94, Box 7480.

openly for the departure of friends and lovers, for not a few bore within their bodies the illegitimate children of American servicemen. To the stirring beat of a military band the seven thousand men paraded for the last time through the streets of Veracruz. The army transports had been moved into the harbor during the night and were tied up all across the waterfront from the great pier number four to the Fiscal wharves. Down Montesinos, down Morelos, and across the broad plaza swung the marching men. Smoothly and without incident the troops were embarked. By 2 p.m. the last American was aboard, and the ships weighed anchor. Within an hour the vessels could barely be seen by the crowds of Mexicans who now lined the stone coping of the waterfront.[21]

Behind the Americans, and almost as an anticlimax, came the Constitutionalist soldiers of Cándido Aguilar. Their discipline was exemplary. There was no friction. A few shots were fired into the air to celebrate the occasion. During the afternoon Aguilar's officers took over the civil administration, by evening the city was policed by the revolutionaries, and on the following day the customhouse was opened for business. After seven months the city was back under the control of the Mexicans. Soon Carranza arrived with his cabinet and his generals to set up his headquarters for the war with Villa and Zapata. Despite the promises he had made to Woodrow Wilson, he proceeded to punish those who had aided the Americans. His government would employ no one who had worked for the military regime, not even the teachers. A completely new police force was organized. For the next nine months the city of Veracruz was to be—for the Constitutionalists—the capital of the Mexican Republic.[22]

Little by little the populace and the city shucked off

21 Funston, "Report."
22 Silliman to Bryan, April 12, 1915 /14837; *El Pueblo*, December 12, 1914, 3:4, December 21, 1914, 1:7, and December 24, 1914, 1:6-7.

the evidences of American rule. The Constitutionalists did not attempt to restore civil government, preferring to keep Veracruz under revolutionary discipline. Otherwise, old habits were revived. Once again it was necessary to bribe a policeman or a public official to persuade him to do his duty. Graft and corruption corroded the government from the highest to the lowest strata. In their daily life the people returned to well-established customs; the streets grew dirty and the garbage remained uncollected, for the new government had no sanitation department. In the market the screens erected by the Americans rusted and fell apart. They were never replaced. There were no regulations, no inspections. Slowly the *zopilotes* drifted back, as though returning to Elysium, to take up their old haunts on the roofs of the city and on the crosses of the parochial church, on the waterfront and in the market. Truly, Veracruz was back to normal. Within a few weeks it was difficult to tell that the Americans had ever occupied the city.[23]

As for the Americans, the occupation experience was proof that Wilson's determination to recognize only good and moral governments, while admirable in abstract, was impossible in practice. Thereafter, Washington would grant recognition to any regime, however corrupt or authoritarian, capable of maintaining itself in power. That this course has also worked evils—witness the recent too-close ties with Trujillo, Batista, and Pérez Jiménez—does not negate the axiom: Wilson's policy, whatever his intention, was a form of dictation completely unacceptable to the Latin American people. No longer would it be possible to treat them as school children. Rather they were accepted as responsible, mature nations, capable of deciding their own destinies. In the reluctant acceptance of that fact by Woodrow Wilson it is possible to see the seeds of Franklin D. Roosevelt's "Good Neighbor Policy."

[23] From personal conversations with various persons in Veracruz in the summer of 1958.

Essay on Sources

THIS ESSAY DOES NOT pretend to be comprehensive, to name all of the sources available to the historian in this field. It would be pointless to list a great number of books, for, wherever possible, books and other secondary materials were ignored in favor of archival and manuscript collections. A few books proved useful, however, and their influence must be acknowledged. Arthur S. Link's *Woodrow Wilson: The New Freedom* (Princeton, 1956) supersedes all previous works on the American president. It does not render them obsolete, however, and one can still use with profit Ray S. Baker's *Woodrow Wilson, Life and Letters* (Garden City, New York, 1927-1937) and Harley Notter's *The Origins of the Foreign Policy of Woodrow Wilson* (Baltimore, 1937). A recent addition to the scores of books on Wilson is the illuminating account by Cary T. Grayson, *Woodrow Wilson: An Intimate Memoir* (New York, 1960). Dr. Grayson devotes most of his memoir to the later period of Wilson's administration, but he gives insights into the president's attitudes at the crucial time of the Tampico incident and the occupation of Veracruz.

Henry Cabot Lodge, in *The Senate and the League of Nations* (New York, 1925), discusses his relationship with Wilson during the crisis. There is no means of checking the accuracy of his reconstruction of conversations with the president, for his memory may have been charged with the later rancor between the two men, but it has the ring of truth and can be used with caution. Charles W. Thompson's *Presidents I've Known and Two Near Presidents* (Indianapolis, 1929) represents a reporter's jaundiced view of Wilson's stubborn nature.

Concerning American relations with Mexico there is no satisfactory book, that is, no book which uses the available archival and manuscript materials in the two countries. It is doubly unfortunate, therefore, that Philip Lowry's excellent doctoral dissertation at Yale University on Woodrow Wilson's Mexican policy has never been published. Edith O'Shaughnessy's *A Diplomat's Wife in Mexico* (New York, 1916) has for many years been considered a gold mine for the student of Mexican history in this period. And indeed it is, though the gold is somewhat tarnished by the discovery that these are probably not the actual letters of Mrs. O'Shaughnessy. In no case do they distort facts, but a comparison with her letters in the New York Public Library shows conclusively that they have been dressed up (though probably not doctored) for publication. Events and the interpretations of events for this period in Mexico are drawn largely from the author's *The Mexican Revolution, 1914-1915* (Bloomington, Indiana, 1960). A Mexican portrayal of the occupation, Justino M. Palomares, *La Invasión Yanqui* (Mexico City, 1940), is by no means reliable or unprejudiced.

Newspapers of the past are the historian's staff of life. Not that newspapers are always or even consistently accurate. But their reporters have recorded information that would be unobtainable elsewhere, and their stories are indispensable for a complete picture of an era. The *New York Times*, with its excellent index, is, of course, without peer. But for the 1910's the *New York World* is helpful for reflecting the views of Wilson's administration, while the *New York Herald* and the *Washington Post* were strong voices of the opposition. In Mexico, the newspapers of the period were usually factional, with little pretense of objectivity. *La Patria*, *El Imparcial*, *El País*, and *El Inde-*

pendiente were all conservative and pro-Huerta, and they ceased publication when Huerta fell. The English-language *Mexican Herald* also represented the conservative, antirevolutionary view of the American colony in that country. At all times it was critical of Wilson's Mexican policies. During the occupation of Veracruz the *Mexican Herald* moved to the port and was published there. *El Pueblo* and *El Liberal* in Mexico City were mouthpieces for the Carrancistas, while *El Monitor* performed a similar function for the Convention and the Villistas. *La Opinión* was published in Veracruz until the advent of the Constitutionalists in November, 1914, when *El Pueblo* was transferred to that city.

The magazine sources in the two countries also proved fruitful. In Mexico, periodicals such as *El Multicolor* were too closely identified with Huerta's regime and were closed by the victorious revolutionaries in the summer of 1914. *Periódico Oficial de Veracruz,* published by the state government of Veracruz-Llave, printed official releases of Huerta's government. When the Carrancistas took Veracruz, its publication continued, though the name was changed to *Gaceta Oficial de Veracruz.* These periodicals, as well as the many newspapers of the times, can be found in the excellent collection of the Hemeroteca Nacional in Mexico City. In the United States, many magazines manifested an interest in the occupation and sent special correspondents to Veracruz. Worth noting are the *Saturday Evening Post, Collier's, Scribners', Survey,* and *Outlook.* The *Literary Digest* performed a valuable function in giving a consensus of American newspaper comment.

Most of the research on this book was done in archives in Mexico and in the United States, principally in Washington's National Archives, and in various collections of personal papers. In the National Archives, the Departments of State, the Army, the Navy, and the Interior files were most important. The State files used were primarily the 812.00 series (Political Affairs in Mexico). The post records of Tampico, Veracruz, and Mexico City are a valuable supplement, however, for they give additional information not included in the State files. In the State section there are also several bound volumes of Wilson-Bryan correspondence. All of the State papers are in good order and well organized and indexed. This is not, unfortunately, true of the Navy and Army files. The unwary researcher needs an Ariadne to find his way through the maze of classifications in these sections, for materials are deposited in record groups, area and subject files, roller drawers, etc., without any apparent consistency. The personnel in charge know their business, though, so that all is not lost.

The author had some difficulty in the Army section, when all documents marked "confidential" were systematically pulled out by an attendant, although all reason for such classification had long since disappeared. But that was in the days of Senator McCarthy's influence, and more recently most of the Army materials for the years before 1945 have been declassified. There was no similar difficulty in using Navy or State files on 1914, for these were completely open to access. Of special note in the Navy files were the logbooks and record signal books for all of the ships in the Atlantic Fleet. The Department of the Navy has kept some records, such as those of the General Board, under its own control. These may be consulted, though the notes taken will be censored, in a warehouse in Alexandria, Virginia.

The use of archival materials in Mexico presented a special problem. The Archivo General de la Nación contained documents only for the pre-1910 period, and other, more recent, records were in private hands. General Roque González Garza, for example, has the most complete documentation on the Convention of Aguascalientes. Surprisingly, there was no trouble involved in using the archive of Defensa Nacional, though a letter of identification from the American embassy was required. Records there seem to be in good order. The author had no success in entering the archives of Foreign Relations. There is a fifty-year rule, and although it is not always enforced, its elasticity is governed by the nature of the specific project. The topic of the occupation of Veracruz—still a touchy subject in Mexico—did not prove to be the "open sesame" to these files. In lieu of using the Foreign Relations archives, therefore, one must resort to government publications in Mexico, such as the *Diario Oficial,* or the State Department papers in Washington.

There is no dearth of personal manuscript collections bearing on the period. The Woodrow Wilson papers in the Library of Congress are at first glance indispensable. But it must be admitted that Wilson's correspondence is disappointing. Rarely does he give any clue in his letters as to his motivation. The president was not a confiding man, not even to his intimate friend, Colonel Edward House. Nonetheless, the House papers at Yale University are required reading for any study of Wilson. In his diary especially, House recorded his day-by-day conversations with the president. Among the various collections in the Library of Congress the Josephus Daniels papers, the William Jennings Bryan papers, and the Ray S. Baker papers were found to be useful, though of secondary importance. Baker's papers are the letters, interviews, etc., which he collected in preparing his massive biography of Wilson, and contain little that has not been utilized in published form. Three other minor collections are worthy of mention: the O'Shaughnessy papers in the New York Public Library, and the William F. Buckley and Emilio Rabasa papers at the University of Texas. The O'Shaughnessy papers are weak on the Mexican period and refer mostly to his diplomatic career in Europe. The Buckley and Rabasa papers deal with the A.B.C. mediation attempt.

Finally, no historian of wars or diplomacy can afford to bury himself in the letters, the dispatches, or the military orders and reports, which have been growing brittle and gathering dust in archives and libraries. These are no adequate substitute for the actual scene of the events. The author visited, therefore, both Tampico and Veracruz. In each city there were chats with "old timers" who remembered (with varying degrees of exactness) the crisis of 1914. He tramped the streets, exploring old buildings, sat under the Portales with the Veracruzanos. In Tampico there was the task of finding the Iturbide Bridge and of identifying the site of the arrest of the sailors. Observations were made of the Pánuco River, of the terrain around Tampico, largely urbanized today, and of the beach at La Barra, whose blackened sands are now redolent of the oil which floats down the river. At Veracruz there was a boat ride to the island of San Juan de Ulua and a descent into the dungeons of the prison. Much has been changed in Veracruz. It is a modern city, with new and taller buildings, with an airport, and it is clean (in comparison with earlier times) and bustling with trade. The vultures have gone forever. There are no prisoners at San Juan de Ulua. But the sea is the same, and the sky, the breakwaters, the granite seawall, the hills, the rains, the Pico de Orizaba, the birds at the waterfront, the old romantic houses. These also are the stuff from which histories are written.

Index

Agramonte, Nicolás de, 83
Aguascalientes, Mexico, 164, 166
Aguilar, General Cándido, 159, 161, 163, 168, 170
Aguilar, Higinio, 169
Alger, William E., 109
Anderson, Captain Edwin A., 101
Arbol Grande, Mexico, 7, 12, 15, 16
Argumedo, Benjamin, 169
Arms shipments: embargo on, 4; aboard the *Ypiranga*, 69-70, 74, 76, 86, 88, 90, 98-99, 150-52
Army, U. S.: mobilized for possible use in Mexico, 62; arrival of in Veracruz, 105-7; and military government of Veracruz, 123-55 *passim*; withdrawal of from Veracruz, 159-63, 165, 168-70
Army Corps of the Northeast, 4, 5
Army Corps of the Northwest, 3, 5
Azcarraga, Mariano, 150
Associated Press, 40, 123
Atlantic Fleet: ordered to Mexico, 51, 53; in Mexican waters, 62, 63; ordered to Tampico, 68; arrives in Veracruz, 99-100; mentioned, 85

Badger, Vice Admiral Charles T.: ordered to Mexico, 53; ordered to Tampico, 68; takes fleet to Veracruz, 73, 85, 86; and the occupation of Veracruz, 100, 101, 106, 113
Bartlett, Ensign Harold Terry, 20
Becerril, General Luis B., 91
Bernstorff, J. H. von, 98
Blanquet, General Aurelio, 91-92
Blockade of Veracruz, 125-26
Blythe, Samuel G., 115

Brooklyn Navy Yard, 115
Bryan, William Jennings: and the Tampico crisis, 17-18, 28, 41-53 *passim*, 61-68 *passim*; limitations of, 31; and the cablegram incident, 56-57; and decision to occupy Veracruz, 76-77; and arms shipment to Huerta, 98-99; and the Constitutionalists, 116, 117; and evacuation of Veracruz, 163, 168
Buckley, William F., 105
Bullfights, 147, 148
Butler, Major S. D., 68

Caballeros, General Luis, 11-12
Cablegram incident, 56-57
Canada, William W.: and the arrested seaman incident, 55; and arms shipment, 69-70, 76; and occupation of Veracruz, 86-90, 97, 103; on American justice, 140; and evacuation of Veracruz, 168, 169
Cardoso de Oliveira, J. M., 109, 159, 163
Carothers, George, 116, 117
Carranza, Venustiano: and Constitutionalist revolution, 3, 5, 6; attitude of toward U. S., 115-18; and currency, 154, 159; feud with Villa, 156-58, 166-67; and the evacuation of Veracruz, 159-65 *passim*, 167-68, 170; and split among the Constitutionalists, 166-67; takes Veracruz, 169, 170
Casualties, 1, 95, 100, 102-3
Cerrillo, Colonel Albino Rodríguez. *See* Rodríguez Cerrillo, Colonel Albino
Chapultepec Castle, 60

Chester, 10, 26, 46, 73, 99, 101
Chihuahua, state of, 4, 5
Coahuila, state of, 3
Collier's Magazine, 102, 123
Comarca Lagunera, Mexico, 5
Connecticut, 10, 11, 73
Constitutionalists: leadership of, 3-6; attack Tampico, 6, 7, 11-19, 47; attitude of toward U. S., 115-18; currency of, 149, 154, 159; feuding among, 156-58, 165-67; and evacuation of Veracruz, 159-65; enter Veracruz, 169, 170-71; mentioned, 41, 69
Contreras, Lt. Colonel Manuel, 91, 92, 94, 99, 103
Convention, 164, 166-67
Copp, Ensign Charles C., 21-23, 24, 25
Correspondents, press, 123, 128
Cortés, Hernán, 83
Courts, 140-44
Courts martial, 144
Crime, 139-40, 141
Currency: problems of in Veracruz, 148-49, 153-54; Constitutionalist, 149, 154, 159
Customs service, 149-54, 162

Daniels, Josephus: and Admiral Mayo, 9-10; and Tampico crisis, 46, 69; and occupation of Veracruz, 70-71, 76-77, 85, 106, 107; statement on withdrawal from Tampico, 112-13; mentioned, 55, 101
Davis, Richard Harding, 123, 126-28
De Agramonte, Nicolás. *See* Agramonte, Nicolás de
De Gaff, Laurent. *See* Gaff, Laurent de
De Oliveira, J. M. Cardoso. *See* Cardoso de Oliveira, J. M.
Des Moines, 11, 17, 43, 46
Díaz, General Porfirio, 6, 14, 84, 88, 106, 142
Disease, 122-23, 129, 136
Division of the North, 3, 5, 159, 167
Dolphin, 11, 14, 15, 19, 23, 46, 48, 68, 70, 71, 73

Doña Cecilia, Mexico, 12, 15, 16
Doughty, Captain H. M., 111
Drake, Sir Francis, 83
Dresden, 13, 111
Duties, customs, 152, 153-54, 160, 161, 168
Dysentery, 129, 136

Earle, Lt. Commander Ralph K., 15, 20, 23, 24
Education, Department of, 144-45
El Imparcial, 107
El Independiente, 107
El Tejar, Mexico, 102, 161, 169
Embargo, 4
Esperanza, 86, 88
Esteva Ruiz, Roberto A., 38, 39, 44, 45
Evacuation of Veracruz, 159-71
Everybody's Magazine, 123

Fabela, Isidro, 165, 167
Figueroa, General Francisco, 91
Finance, Department of, 146, 148
Fiske, Admiral B. A., 9
Fiske, Captain Harold B., 146
Fletcher, Rear Admiral Frank F.: stationed at Veracruz, 8-9; and the Tampico incident, 26-28, 48; and the arrested seaman incident, 55; and occupation of Veracruz, 69, 73, 77, 78, 85, 86, 90, 93, 96-100 *passim*, 103-4, 105, 106; mentioned, 13, 25, 48
Flies, 132, 133
Florida, 9, 85, 86, 89, 94
Food, 125-26, 135, 136
Fuller, Paul, 158-59
Funston, General Frederick: and occupation of Veracruz, 105, 106; and military government of Veracruz, 123-52 *passim;* and evacuation of Veracruz, 160-63 *passim,* 165, 168, 169

Gaff, Laurent de, 83
Gambling concessions, 125, 147, 148
Garbage, 131, 171
Garrison, Lindley M.: and occupation of Veracruz, 76, 104, 106,

Garrison, Lindley M. (*continued*): 107, 123, 126, 140; and arms shipment to Huerta, 152; and evacuation of Veracruz, 160, 161, 162
Gasoline: need for, 19-20; secured from Tryon, 20-23
Giles, Lieutenant W. J., 150
González, Pablo, 4, 5, 6, 117, 119, 167
Grayson, Dr. Cary, 18, 29, 43, 49, 114
Greytown, Nicaragua, 50
Gutiérrez, Eulalio, 166

Hancock, 68, 100
Hanna, William C., 109
Harrington, Seaman J. P., 21, 22
Hawkins, John, 83
Haywood, William, 59
Hermione, 111
Hidalgo, Father Miguel, 108
Hinojosa, Colonel Ramón H., 23, 26, 38, 44, 63
House, Colonel Edward, 77, 114, 115
Huasteca Oil Company, 68, 110
Huerta, General Victoriano: Wilson's attitude toward, 1-2, 3, 5, 8, 30, 36, 37-38, 49, 62, 74, 116; rise to power, 2, 3; and Constitutionalist revolution, 3-5, 41, 115, 116; and John Lind, 32; friendship with the O'Shaughnessys, 37, 45, 51-52, 60; and Tampico crisis, 39-68 *passim;* arms shipment for, 69-70, 74-77 *passim*, 85, 86, 98, 152; breaks diplomatic relations with U. S., 109; and mediation attempts, 117-19; and Richard Harding Davis, 127; and the courts, 143; overthrow of, 149, 157-58; and customs duties, 153-54

International Workers of the World, 59
Ipiranga. See Ypiranga
Isle of Sacrifices, 84
Iturbide, Eduardo, 108
Iturbide Bridge, 16, 18, 19, 20, 38

Juárez, Benito, 96, 156
"Junta of chiefs," 158, 166. *See also* Convention

Kerr, Robert J., 104, 105, 106, 128
Knox, Philander C., 35

"La Galera," 99, 101
Laguna Puerta, 12
Lansing, Robert, 32-33, 50, 118, 151, 161
La Patria, 107
Larue, F. C., 54, 55
Law enforcement, 139-44
League of Nations, 29
Lejeune, Colonel J. A., 68
Lerdo, Miguel, 156
Lerdo, Sebastián, 156-57
Leva, 5
Liberating Army of the South, 167
Libertad, 17
Lind, John, 32, 49, 114
Lodge, Henry Cabot, 73-74, 76
London, Jack, 102, 123
Looting, 150
López Portillo y Rojas, José, 39, 62, 64, 65, 66, 67
Lorencillo, 83
Lottery, 125, 148
Louis Philippe, 84
Luby, Commander J. M., 145

Maass, General Gustavo: and defense of Veracruz, 69, 87, 89, 90, 91; withdrawal of from Veracruz, 92, 93, 96, 97; blockades Veracruz, 125; mentioned, 145
Maass, General Joaquín, 107-8
McAdoo, William G., 29, 50
Madero, Francisco I., 3, 6, 37, 142
Mail service, 145-46, 169
Maine, 59
Malaria, 129, 133
Mare Island Navy Yard, 9
Marine courier, arrest of, 18-19, 24
Marines, U. S.: and occupation of Veracruz, 89, 92-97 *passim*, 100-1, 106-7, 127; and cleanup of Veracruz, 103, 135; mentioned, 150, 169

Market: cleanup of, 130-33; mentioned, 171

Mayo, Rear Admiral Henry T.: in command at Tampico, 8, 10-11; description and career of, 9-10; and Constitutionalist attack on Tampico, 12-18 *passim;* and the Tampico crisis, 23-30 *passim,* 38-39, 40, 42, 43, 50; and plans for occupying Tampico, 46-48, 68-69; ordered to Veracruz, 70-73; and evacuation of Americans from Tampico, 110-13; mentioned, 86

Mazatlán, Mexico, 109

Mediation attempts, 118-19, 143

Mexican Herald, 131

Mexico, 86, 87

Miller, Clarence: and Constitutionalist attack on Tampico, 12, 16, 17; and Tampico crisis, 23-27 *passim;* and evacuation of Americans from Tampico, 47-48, 110-11; and withdrawal from Tampico, 71-72

Miller, Major Charles, 144-45

Minnesota, 10, 54, 100

Moffett, Commander William A., 26, 99, 102

Monterrey, Mexico, 109

Morelos, state of, 3

Morelos Zaragoza, General Ignacio: and defense of Tampico, 7, 11, 14, 15, 47; and arrest of the marine courier, 18-19, 24; and Tampico crisis, 22-27 *passim,* 32, 38, 44, 63; and rioting in Tampico, 110

Mosquitoes, 129, 133

Nafarrete, Colonel Emiliano J., 15

Navy, U. S.: at Tampico, 8, 10-11, 13-19 *passim,* 46-48, 68-73 *passim;* at Veracruz, 8, 69, 73; and occupation of Veracruz, 85-87, 89, 92-97, 99-102. *See also* Atlantic Fleet; Daniels, Josephus

Neville, Colonel W. C., 93

New Hampshire, 101

New York Herald, 52, 55

New York Sun, 52

North Dakota, 135

Obregón, Alvaro: and Constitutionalist revolution, 3-6 *passim,* 117, 119; and the Convention, 166; supports Carranza, 167

Ocampo, Melchor, 156

Occupation. *See under* Veracruz

Oil, in Tampico, 6-7

Oliveira, J. M. Cardoso de. *See* Cardoso de Oliveira, J. M.

O'Shaughnessy, Edith (Mrs. Nelson J.), 34, 36, 37, 39, 45, 51, 56, 60, 80

O'Shaughnessy, Nelson J.: and Tampico crisis, 32, 38-45, 49, 51, 56, 59-67; background and career of, 34-37; friendship with Huerta, 37, 45, 51-52, 60; expelled from Mexico, 109; mentioned, 108

Palmer, Frederick, 123

Pánuco River, 6, 10, 69

Pico de Orizaba, 80

Portillo y Rojas, José López. *See* López Portillo y Rojas, José

Postal service. *See* Mail service

Prairie, 86, 87, 89, 92, 97, 99, 101, 135

Press. *See* Correspondents

Prisons. *See* "La Galera," San Juan de Ulua

Progresso, Mexico, 109

Prostitution, 136-38

Public Safety, Department of, 139, 140

Public Works, Department of, 130, 133-34

Refugees: at Tampico, 17-18, 19, 48, 72; evacuated from Tampico, 111-13; at Veracruz, 87-88, 125, 160-62, 168

Revenue, 146-54 *passim*

Rioting: in Mexico City, 108; elsewhere in Mexico, 109; in Tampico, 110

Robinson, H. M., 145-46

Rodríguez Cerrillo, Colonel Albino, 91, 92, 99, 103

Rojas, José López Portillo y. *See* López Portillo y Rojas, José

Root, Elihu, 35, 74, 76
Roosevelt, Franklin D., 171
Roosevelt, Theodore, 34
Ruhl, Arthur, 123
Ruiz, Roberto A. Esteva. *See* Esteva Ruiz, Roberto A.
Rush, Captain William R., 86, 92, 93

San Francisco, 11, 46, 73, 99, 101, 150
Sanitation: lack of in Veracruz, 81-82, 130, 171; enforcement of, 129-38 *passim*
San Juan del Norte. *See* Greytown
San Juan de Ulua: description of, 78, 80-81; and defense of Veracruz, 87; cleanup of, 134-36; mentioned, 83, 84, 90
Saturday Evening Post, 115
Sayre, Francis B., 29
Schools, 144-45
Scott, General Winfield, 84
Sewage disposal, 133
Siefert, Coxswain G. H., 21, 22
Silliman, John R., 159
Smith, Major Harry A., 139, 140, 142, 143
Soledad, Mexico, 143
South Carolina, 101, 145
Stamps: postage, 146; tax, 147
Stewart, Charles H., 105
Stickney, Commander Herman O.: and occupation of Veracruz, 86, 87; in charge of customs service, 105, 150-53, 162; and evacuation of Veracruz, 168, 169

Taft, William H., 4
Tampico, Mexico: incident at, 1, 3, 19-28, 38-67 *passim;* description of, 6-7; Constitutionalist attack on, 6, 7, 11-19, 47; refugees at, 17-18, 19, 48, 111-13; plans for seizure of, 46-48, 68-69; withdrawal from, 70-73, 110-13; rioting in, 110
Taxes, 146-47, 149
Tejería, Mexico, 92, 96, 97, 101
Tennessee, 9
Thompson, Charles W., 30, 32

Tryon, Max, 19, 21, 22, 23, 24
Tumulty, Joseph, 30, 64
Tyrrell, Sir William, 2

Ultimatum, Mayo's, 25-27, 38-39, 40, 42, 44, 50, 61
United Press, 123
Uribe, Virgilio, 97
Utah, 85, 86, 89, 96, 98, 149

Venereal disease, 136-37
Veracruz, Mexico: occupation of, 1, 85-120; arms shipment to, 69-70, 74, 76, 86, 88, 90, 98-99, 150-51; decision to occupy, 70-77; description and history of, 78-85; conditions in under occupation, 121-55; evacuation of, 159-71
Veracruz, 12, 13, 15, 16
Veracruz-Llave, state of, 147, 148
Vermont, 101
Villa, Francisco: and Constitutionalist revolution, 3, 4, 5, 6, 12, 119, 159, 168, 169, 170; attitude toward U. S., 116-17; feud with Carranza, 156-58, 166-67; mentioned, 74, 123
Vogelsang, C. T., 99
Von Bernstorff, J. H. *See* Bernstorff, J. H. von
Vultures. *See Zopilotes*

Wakiva, 68, 110, 111
Washington Post, 52
Water station, 102, 161, 169
Wilson, Eleanor, 29, 114
Wilson, Ellen Axson (Mrs. Woodrow), 28, 66, 114
Wilson, Henry Lane, 31, 36, 37
Wilson, Woodrow: attitude toward Huerta, 1-2, 3, 5, 8, 30, 36, 37-38, 49, 62, 74, 116; Mexican policy of, 2, 30, 31, 38, 105, 171; support for policies of, 3, 57-59, 113; attitude toward Americans in Mexico, 18, 72, 74, 113; and Tampico crisis, 25, 28, 30, 32-33, 43, 48-68 *passim*, political philosophy of, 29-30; lack of understanding of Mexican problems, 30-32, 55, 74; and

Woodrow Wilson (*continued*):
arrested seaman incident, 55; and the decision to occupy Veracruz, 70, 73-77; and occupation of Veracruz, 90, 92, 104-5, 107, 114-16; and the Constitutionalists, 115-18, 158-59; and mediation attempts, 118-19; insists on peace in Mexico, 123, 126, 128; and the evacuation of Veracruz, 161-65 *passim;* mentioned, 4, 151, 152, 155, 170
Wolf, Major Paul A., 130, 133

Ypiranga, 76, 86, 87, 88, 90, 98-99, 150-52

Zapata, Emiliano, 3, 12, 158, 166, 167, 168, 169, 170
Zaragoza, General Ignacio Morelos. *See* Morelos Zaragazo, General Ignacio
Zaragoza, 13, 15, 17, 111
Zayas, Major Diego, 93
Zopilotes, 79, 81, 82, 93, 103, 130-32, 171